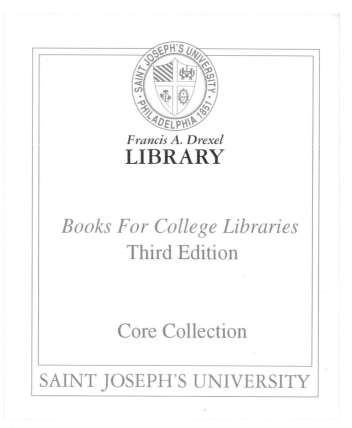

POLICY STUDIES IN EMPLOYMENT AND WELFARE NUMBER 39

General Editor: Sar A. Levitan

Working for the Sovereign

Employee Relations in the Federal Government

Sar A. Levitan
Alexandra B. Noden

THE JOHNS HOPKINS UNIVERSITY PRESS
Baltimore and London

This study was prepared under a grant from the Ford Foundation.

© 1983 by The Johns Hopkins University Press
Printed in the United States of America

The Johns Hopkins University Press, Baltimore, Maryland 21218
The Johns Hopkins Press Ltd, London

Library of Congress Cataloging in Publication Data

Levitan, Sar A.
  Working for the sovereign.

  (Policy studies in employment and welfare; no. 39)
  Includes index.
  1. Collective bargaining—Government employees—
United States. 2. Civil service—United States—
Personnel management. 3. Employee-management relations
in government—United States. 4. United States—
Officials and employees. I. Noden, Alexandra B.
II. Title. III. Series.
HD8005.6.U5L479   1983   353.001   82-49064
ISBN 0-8018-3028-1

Contents

Preface

The Reagan administration has initiated radical changes in the functions of the federal government. These changes may have a pervasive impact upon the structure of the federal civil service and the administration of employee relations in the federal establishment. An analysis of the management of the federal civil service and the shifts it is experiencing as a result of the Reagan administration changes appeared, therefore, timely, particularly since no review of employee relations in the federal government has appeared for some time.

Nearly a century has elapsed since the federal government attempted to establish a stable civil service system based on merit but which is responsive to changing political leadership. Although the system has never been completely free of political intervention and manipulation by elected officials and politically appointed managers, during the past twenty years considerable progress in the development of unions and a machinery aimed at protecting the rights of individual federal employees had occurred.

Some observers have expressed concerns that the Reagan administration may be reversing this trend. The changes instituted during its first eighteen months, including trimming the size of the federal labor force, has not only caused serious deterioration of morale but has also opened the administration to charges of attempting to politicize the federal civil service system.

Private sector models of labor-management relations have served as a central reference point in the debate over the appropriate structure of employee relations in the federal establishment. While it is clear that unique aspects of employment in the federal government cannot be ignored, the differences from private employment and the significance of political leaders' roles as sovereigns have frequently been exaggerated. The private sector system of collective bargaining cannot be imposed *in toto* onto the federal establishment, but the justifications for restricting worker rights and labor-management negotiations are often weaker than they first appear.

In some areas, the refusal to adopt private sector models of employee relations has caused serious problems within the federal civil service. The pay structure for federal employees is in a state of disarray largely because successive administrations and congresses have refused to bargain over wages or to peg federal pay to remuneration received by workers performing similar duties in the private sector. In the absence of a system that guarantees civil servants market-level compensation, federal salaries in the higher levels of the civil service have fallen significantly behind those for comparable positions in the private sector, and the ensuing poor morale has led to an exodus of top managers from the federal establishment, thereby endangering the efficient performance and delivery of vital federal services.

Wherever collective bargaining has been permitted in the federal government, it has served well. Current procedures, albeit limited in scope, have proven effective in resolving employee grievances and in arbitrating contract disputes. On the basis of this experience, the federal government might do well to take a leaf out of private sector employee relations and expand the scope of collective bargaining in the federal establishment.

A departure from private sector employee practices is essential, however, with regard to hiring and firing of federal employees. Because of the dangers that political leaders will seek to manipulate the civil service for political ends, management discretion in hiring and firing must be much narrower than that enjoyed by private employers. Objective entrance examinations and promotion criteria have played an important role in shielding civil servants from partisan pressures while ensuring that the system is fair and effective in maintaining a qualified work force. For this reason, management's appeals for greater flexibility in areas of hiring and firing must be greeted with caution.

Virtually all sides in the debate over federal employee relations acknowledge that a hybrid structure only partially rooted in private sector experience is required. The disturbing conclusion of this study is that private sector analogies are utilized in the current structure of federal employee relations in a manner nearly opposite to that which logic would seem to dictate. In questions of worker rights and compensation, where the distinctions between public and private sectors are seldom convincing and often counterproductive, political leaders have repeatedly refused to adopt collective bargaining procedures based on private sector models. In issues of hiring and firing, where federal civil service practices appear most unique, private sector experiences are evoked in an attempt to demonstrate that broader discretion for political appointees is necessary to ensure greater flexibility and efficiency. If employee relations in the federal establishment are to be placed back on the right track, this pattern and use of private sector models should be used only when appropriate rather than when expedient.

To summarize, the present study reviews the structure of federal management and the rise of federal unions during the past two decades. It then examines the climate of collective bargaining that has developed during the period and the role that neutrals, or peace keepers, play in the settlement of labor-management disputes in the federal establishment. The study next considers the machinery used to determine the pay and fringe benefits of federal workers. It closes with an analysis of the various attempts that have been used to rationalize the federal hiring, promotion, and firing procedures.

Numerous participants in federal employee relations have been helpful in the preparation of this study. I am particularly grateful to Gregory Ahart, General Accounting Office; Ellen Bussy, Personnel Appeals Board, General Accounting Office; Henry Frazier, Federal Labor Relations Authority; Stanley Gordon, Public Employee Department, AFL-CIO; David Green, Department of Defense; Ronald Haughton, Federal Labor Relations Authority; Anthony Ingrassia, Office of Personnel Management; Marc Rosenbloom, Equal Employment Opportunity Commission; and Howard Solomon, Federal Service Impasses Panel. They are all, of course, absolved of any errors of omission and commission but they have all helped improve the final product.

Beth Noden, who collaborated on the research of this study, left before the final draft was completed to pursue the study of law and should not be held responsible for the conclusions. I am indebted to Clifford M. Johnson for his thoughtful and extensive contributions to the final draft and to Bobby Webster for the final touches in preparing the manuscript for publication.

The study was prepared under an ongoing grant from the Ford Foundation to the Center for Social Policy Studies of the George Washington University. In accordance with the foundation's practice, complete responsibility for the preparation of the volume was left to me.

Sar A. Levitan

Working for the Sovereign

1

Managing in the Public Interest

Managing the federal work force would pose a challenge for even the most talented administrator. As the nation's largest employer, the federal government maintains a combined total of more than 2 million Americans on its civilian payrolls. Its employees span virtually every occupational category, from janitors and filing clerks to engineers and astronomers, and are dispersed throughout the country in a myriad different agencies. The federal work force is united by little more than the common source of its paycheck, rendering even the most basic initiatives affecting employment relations cumbersome and unwieldy.

Yet the management problems of the federal employment system stem from troubles much deeper than its size and complexity. The Congress and the nation's chief executive, who serve as the government's "board of directors" in setting management policies, are faced with additional obstacles and handicaps without parallel in the private sector. They are forced to play dual and often conflicting roles, responding in a traditional sense to administrative goals of efficient organization while at the same time serving as representatives of the people and conduits for expression of the popular will. As a result, the White House and Congress continually mediate disputes between competing interest groups with diverse goals, some of which have no relevance to the smooth and efficient management of the federal work force. While private sector managers must also deal with issues unrelated to efficiency, they are not saddled with the responsibilities encountered regularly by federal politicians and administrators.

In federal employee relations management must serve two distinct functions. When possible, federal executives have sought to act as traditional managers, attempting to develop bureaucratic arrangements that standardize the personnel system and establish procedures for resolving conflict. In this sense, aspects of the federal employment system have been modeled after practices followed in the private sector. Yet this traditional management role cannot be maintained when more is at issue than the balance between efficiency and worker rights. As outside interest groups intervene, federal policymakers are forced to seek fundamentally political solutions to problems associated with the federal work force, and management options become severely constrained by the need to minimize political conflict and reconcile disparate goals.

The vulnerability of federal managers to political pressures has also created special problems for federal employees. Civil service statutes, which institutionalize federal employment practices, provide federal employees some job security protection. In more recent years, measured steps toward collective bargaining have also given unions modest leverage in promoting the rights and interests of federal workers. By offering labor leaders a small voice in agency policies and a platform from which to air employee concerns, the adaptation of traditional labor-management structures found in the private sector has shielded federal employees somewhat from the vicissitudes of political change.

It remains unclear whether the steady gains of federal employees toward negotiations and a meaningful role in shaping their working conditions will continue in the years ahead. Narrow issues in federal employment are now routinely resolved through collective bargaining mechanisms, but attempts to rationalize more controversial matters of compensation, hiring, and firing appear to be faltering in the early 1980s. More importantly, the growing popularity of attacking federal activities has fueled sustained attacks on the federal bureaucracy, thrusting pay, employee selection, and even basic job security concerns into heated political battles.

The Rise of a Civil Service

In virtually all developed nations, efforts have been made to develop a professional work force that tends competently to government affairs while providing some continuity during changes in the political leadership. The rise of a civil service resulted from the struggle of striking a balance between the protection of government employees from capricious action and assurances of continuing responsiveness to the directives of political leaders. Regardless of culture or type of government, the systems that have emerged share common structural elements and have been subject to perennial criticism for fostering job security rather than professionalism and efficiency.

In the United States, the push for reforming the federal employment spoils system based solely on political patronage gained momentum following the Civil War and the consequent growth of the national government. The assassination of President James Garfield by a disgruntled federal job seeker in 1881 focused dissatisfaction with the disruptive elements of the patronage system, and created a political environment conducive to the wholesale reorganization of federal hiring practices. In 1883 the Pendleton Act established the federal civil service along with its guiding principle of merit, which remains the cornerstone of the system a century later.

In attempting to replace campaign "hacks" with professional civil servants, the Pendleton Act loosened the ties between federal executives and their employees. The merit concept restricted the president's ability to reward supporters and ensure bureaucratic loyalty by removing the chief executive from direct involvement in rewarding loyal employees with higher pay and improved working conditions. Civil servants had the advantages of greater job security and a more orderly process of hiring and promotions, but they also were more easily ignored by presidents and members of Congress, who had no personal commitment to their well-being.

The establishment of a civil service was based on the notion that federal employees should be kept outside the political system, although the temptations of the old-fashioned spoils system reemerged from time to time. Presidents Theodore Roosevelt and William Taft went so far as to impose "gag" orders to prevent federal workers from pressing their wage or other demands beyond agency boundaries. In passing the 1912 Lloyd-LaFollette Act which guaranteed federal employees the right to petition the Congress directly, legislators corrected this abridgment of civil rights but preserved the goal of a nonpolitical civil service. The adoption of the Hatch Act in 1939 was a further attempt to prevent the politicization of the federal work force. The law sought to "protect"

3

civil servants from coercion and intimidation by prohibiting them from participating actively in federal election campaigns or from providing organizational support to candidates.

The emphasis on a nonpartisan civil service has played an essential role in developing a sense of common interest among employees of the federal government. Once freed from allegiances to political leaders, federal workers gradually came to recognize the requirement of protection and representation through new channels of collective action. Whereas the beneficiaries of political patronage had been saddled with higher loyalties, the burgeoning class of civil servants began to view its self-interest in ways akin to employees in the private sector. In this context, it is hardly surprising that sizable portions of the federal work force turned to unions as a means of promoting their interests in the civil service system.

The organization of civil servants was originally hindered by the absence of any explicit provisions for unions within the federal government, a barrier that was not removed until 1962 when President John F. Kennedy signed an executive order affirming the rights of employees to form and join unions. Since that time, federal unions have expanded to the point where they now represent three of every five federal employees. Although union bargaining rights are sharply restricted, organized labor in the federal sector has become a significant force influencing employee relations in the federal establishment.

Fragments of Collective Bargaining

Before 1962, there was no systematic provision for federal collective bargaining, although unions and some agency managers did meet informally to discuss matters of mutual interest. The "bread and butter" issues—pay, fringe benefits, classification, and job description—were unchallenged management prerogatives. The only recourse for unions wishing to have an impact on these issues was lobbying, since there were no institutional arrangements for dealing with worker concerns relating to personnel policy and practice.

Increasingly, the Congress and the executive agencies recognized a need for greater uniformity in federal policy to deal with the unionization of the rapidly growing bureaucracy and the proliferating labor units. These concerns were strengthened by political pressures from federal workers and outside unions to provide some framework for organized labor in the federal government. The private sector model of collective bargaining appeared to furnish a simple and attractive basis for responding to both management and labor objectives.

The 1962 executive order issued by President Kennedy was responsive to these pressures. It opened the door to collective bargaining as a means of resolving marginal disputes between management and labor. The scope of bargaining authorized in the order fell far short, however, of the private sector model: wages and fringe benefits, hiring, work assignments, disciplinary actions, contracting out, and firing all remained federal management rights. Yet the establishment of the bargaining process and its reaffirmation by President Richard M. Nixon's executive order in 1969 did bolster the legitimacy of unions as representing valid worker interests. During the past two decades unions have lobbied aggressively for further expansion of recognized bargaining rights.

The Civil Service Reform Act of 1978, although conceived by President Jimmy Carter as a means of streamlining the federal bureaucracy and bolstering management efficiency, also brought modest gains for organized labor in its pursuit of a federal collective bargaining system. The act not only gave legislative sanction to collective bargaining but also created new opportunities for unions to expand the scope of negotiations. The law widened the scope of bargaining and enhanced the role of the neutral interpretive agency, giving the bargaining process increased importance as a means by which unions protect the job rights and dignity of their members.

These changes in limits on negotiability provide significant new footholds for federal unions, but they also serve as reminders of how little the 1978 Civil Service Reform Act altered the basic structure of federal employee relations. While the Carter administration tried to sell its proposed overhaul of the civil service as a thoroughgoing reform, it failed to touch on most key union concerns. It did not alter the federal salary structure, or the methods by which federal wages were set and positions classified. It rejected the idea of expanding the union role in government by refusing to guarantee collective bargaining rights over wages and fringe benefits. In sum, the reform bill was conceived and intended largely as a management tool to promote greater efficiency and flexibility in the civil service, and the limited concessions in collective bargaining and arbitration rights were attempts more to defuse union opposition than to address labor's own objectives.

The justification for severe restrictions on the scope of collective bargaining in the federal sector continues to be a source of considerable debate. The absence of market cost-benefit calculations by which to measure compensation for federal employees has been noted countless times, and yet because of constituent pressures on the Congress management will probably bargain hard at the negotiating table to protect the taxpayers' interest. A "sovereignty" argument also supports narrow bargaining rights and a ban on federal strikes; presumably the sovereign government, as representative of the popular will, has the unassailable right to act unilaterally and is to be obeyed rather than challenged. The claim that bargaining rights are antithetical to the public interest is unconvincing, and in any case federal employees are unlikely to accept this view. As former Secretary of Labor Willard Wirtz stressed, "This doctrine is wrong in theory; what's more, it won't work."[1]

Whether out of concern for the public interest or merely out of a desire to preserve management prerogatives, the decision makers have consistently denied federal workers numerous rights enjoyed by employees in the private sector. Unions of federal employees can engage in collective bargaining over various administrative issues, but cannot, in all but a few agencies, raise the key matter of compensation at the negotiating table. Federal workers do not have the right to strike, and many forms of political activity remain proscribed under the Hatch Act. Federal unions can seek gains only at the margin, generally lacking the clout to secure significant victories. Even if many of the restrictions placed on unions reflect concern, real or imaginary, for the efficiency of federal operations, the result is the handicapping of collective action by federal workers.

Today's provocative question is to what extent issues in federal employee relations could be addressed through collective bargaining, thereby granting to federal workers some greater role in shaping their employment conditions. In areas in which conflict is limited to employees and their supervisors (e.g., aspects of contract negotiation and administration), traditional collective bargaining practices have proven fairly successful in resolving disputes. The gains have not been extended to broader controversial issues, leaving the key terms of employment to determination by fiat through political channels. If collective bargaining could be extended effectively to issues of compensation, hiring, and firing, elected officials would continue to be responsible for preventing dramatic departures from the popular will and public interest. Federal workers for the first time would be granted a legitimate place in an orderly labor relations system, shielded from the extremes of political expediency, and able to influence their work futures.

Determining a Fair Day's Pay

Although wages are generally non-negotiable in the federal sector, attempts have been made to establish a fair and independent mechanism for setting federal pay outside political realms. In the absence of market mechanisms to establish wage levels, these efforts have focused on the concept of "comparability" as the basis for determining federal compensation. The concept assumes that the government should follow rather than lead wage trends in the private sector, and that the civil service will be able to retain adequate numbers of qualified people without significantly influencing pay scales in the broader labor market. No attempt is made to assess the relative fairness of the particular wage rates in the private sector; the goal is to establish internally equitable classification systems which accurately mirror private wage rates as standards for "just pay."

The comparability principle was developed in response to complaints by federal employees that federal pay lagged significantly behind that of private industry. The concept carried great political appeal, for it allowed the Congress to shift controversies regarding pay to the executive branch while putting forth a standard of equity that appeared eminently reasonable. As noted by the former director of the Office of Personnel Management, comparability also added a sense of objectivity and regularity to the federal pay structures, providing an "objective, quantifiable measure of the result of the interplay of market forces" and "contributing to stability of employee expectations about the timing of pay adjustments, and to the Government's need to plan on the timing and approximate size of pay adjustments."[2]

These arguments proved persuasive enough to ensure adoption of the comparability principle in 1962, but its implementation has raised a host of problems. By using private sector pay as its baseline, comparability assumes a rough equivalence between positions in the federal government and the larger labor market which may not exist. The comparability system also may sanction wage inequities linked to sex, race, or occupational biases. Finally, many of the technical questions associated with the implementation of comparability, ranging from the selection of valid private sector samples for comparison to the treatment of fringe benefits and possible intangible advantages of federal employment, have defied easy resolution. Equitable wage rates flow neither easily nor directly from the concept of comparability alone, in spite of its simplistic appeal.

These theoretical and administrative struggles might be manageable, were it not for the highly visible nature of federal compensation. As budget outlooks have worsened in recent years, obvious targets for public frustrations have been the burdens of federal taxation and the role of the federal bureaucracy. Basing pay scales on comparability surveys ignores the changing attitudes and competing demands of taxpayers, and thus has come into increasing conflict with political pressures to limit compensation for federal workers. Predictably, politicians have responded by abandoning comparability as a guiding or overriding principle in establishing federal salary levels. Federal wage rates remain more a function of prevailing economic conditions, political climate, and the effectiveness of federal unions than of statutory provisions to ensure comparability with the private sector.

Federal unions continue to refer to the concept of comparability in justifying demands for higher pay, but they do not expect administrative mechanisms to dictate wage rates in any independent way. Recognizing that labor relations in the federal sector are subject to political interventions, the unions have consistently focused the majority of their resources in lobbying efforts. In fact, given the extremely narrow range of issues that can be addressed through collective bargaining, the clout of political lobbying may be the only reason why many federal employees join and contribute to unions. There is little hope that questions of interest to federal workers will ever be removed totally from political spheres, and they will continue to have no choice but to deal with the White House and the Congress both as traditional managers and as their duly elected representatives.

The quasipolitical nature of federal employee relations poses unique problems for management as well as labor, in that concerns for efficiency and sound administration are often ignored amid more powerful political demands. For example, pay ceilings imposed on senior executives have made it increasingly difficult to retain the most qualified and experienced federal workers, even though high turnover in these upper managerial ranks is recognized as a serious threat to the efficiency of the system. Perceptions that the government is not fulfilling its pledge of comparability with the private sector, or that it is restricting opportunities for promotions, can also undermine morale and increase obstacles to the development of a competent civil service. Elected officials always have the option of moderating pay hikes in the face of strident taxpayer demands, but such compromises are seldom achieved without a price.

An Assault on Established Rules

Compensation is not the only area of federal employee relations in which political leaders face disparate or even contradictory goals. Criteria for hiring and firing in the federal sector have emerged during the past decade as focal points for sharp political conflict. Whether in hiring procedures to promote social equity or federal layoffs to further budgetary goals, interest groups have seized upon these issues with little or no concern for the needs of federal managers or the rights of federal workers. The resulting conflicts within the federal establishment are necessarily resolved in political realms without the participation of employee representatives. More disturbing for federal workers is the inherent danger of enlarging management prerogatives in response to such controversies, undermining not only job security but also merit principles which form the foundation of the civil service.

Efforts to alter the composition of the federal work force have begun not as challenges to worker protections; diverse constituencies have simply attempted to secure preferential treatment by flexing their political muscle and appealing to broader social goals. For women and minorities, such appeals frequently have been directed to the promotion of social equity and the reversal of past patterns of employment discrimination. For veterans, preferential claims have been rooted in calls for gratitude. These wide-ranging political demands share a common approach—they all seek to mold federal employment to serve ends outside the scope of strict efficiency, and reject the notion of merit as the sole criterion for selecting federal employees.

Because the merit principle lies at the heart of the civil service system, much of the controversy regarding federal hiring practices has focused upon standardized entrance exams used to screen job applicants for professional, administrative, and clerical positions. While the validity of the tests as measures of future competence continues to be debated, there is no question that blacks taking the exams have fared far worse proportionately than whites. Certainly the absence of compelling evidence that test results accurately predict job performance made a persuasive case for revision of federal hiring procedures to set an example of equal opportunity for private employers. The difficulty of balancing goals of merit hiring and affirmative action heightened the problems associated with the development of an entrance exam to fill large numbers of diverse jobs in a fair and efficient manner. Pressured by a court order, the Reagan administration abandoned the standardized professional, administrative, and clerical entrance (PACE) exams and thereby reopened the prospect of hiring linked to political ideology instead of merit principles.

If other entrance exams are abolished, future policies toward veterans and women in federal hiring may be affected. Since 1944, the federal government has extended hiring preferences to veterans as a form of compensation for their service or disabilities, a policy that has hindered the entrance and advancement of nonveterans, and particularly of women, in the federal work force. With the growing militancy of women's organizations during the 1970s, veterans' preferences were scaled back somewhat, but President Reagan has expressed a renewed commitment to special treatment for veterans. It is not clear how the administration will implement this preference in the absence of standardized examination scores, and the concept of favoring veterans may serve only to expand managerial discretion in federal hiring.

The drive to reduce the size of the federal work force has posed direct threats to the rights and interests of federal workers, and has drawn new attention to civil service procedures governing reductions in force (RIFs). Civil service rules restrict management in firing workers and offer employees with greatest seniority the opportunity to move into other jobs when their positions are eliminated. The system of last-hired, first-fired makes recent gains of women and minorities highly vulnerable to overall cuts in the federal work force. Veterans' preferences provide an extra measure of protection to employees with some military service while exposing nonveterans to a disproportionate share of the risks of federal layoffs. Because statutes restrict flexibility in terminating unnecessary personnel, administration officials contemplate legislative changes to give greater weight to performance evaluations than to seniority in firing decisions.

The Options Ahead

Unions have been slow to react to the underlying threats presented by the broader social demands to overhaul existing personnel practices. Representing the employed rather than prospective applicants, unions have prudently avoided the controversy regarding entrance examinations and their effects on equal opportunity. Counting among their members both veterans and women, the unions have been equally reticent with regard to veterans' hiring preferences and their impact by gender. Federal unions have opposed the RIFs initiated by the Reagan administration, but they have demonstrated little clout in the sweeping budget debates from which the cuts emanated and they have avoided battles with private sector unions over issues of contracting practices. Whether this relative complacency is disrupted will depend on how vigorously the Reagan administration pursues greater management discretion at the expense of basic worker rights offered by existing civil service rules.

Within a confined framework, federal workers have fought a long, uphill battle to secure some rights to influence the terms of their employment. The past two decades have brought considerable progress in this regard, as the growth of federal unions and the gradual, albeit marginal, expansion of collective bargaining rights have given federal employees modest leverage over management actions. Yet even when labor-management disputes might be settled by negotiations, the sovereign powers of government have often enhanced the temptation to manage unilaterally rather than seeking to reconcile labor and management views. The Reagan administration in particular seems prepared to reverse past gains in worker rights as it pursues greater flexibility and discretion in addressing its own concerns.

In assessing the development of the federal employment system, it is important to ask whether the settlement of labor-management differences responds adequately to the unique elements of the federal establishment. Political leaders justify deviations from private sector practices as necessary adjustments to the federal government's special circumstances, yet there is considerable evidence that the politicized nature of federal employment exacts sizable costs in the loss of experienced workers, low morale, and poor organization. The crucial question is whether some portion of these costs is avoidable, and whether alternative federal employment relations arrangements could better serve both labor and management goals in the public interest.

2

The Rise of Federal Unions

The organization of federal employees into unions was an essential first step toward greater protection of individual rights in the federal government. The rise of an independent civil service provided a basis for common interest among federal workers, but the plethora of civil service regulations and a lingering ethic of submissiveness and obedience to political leaders slowed organizing efforts in the bureaucracy. While the rights of employees to bargain collectively through their representatives was generally accepted in the private sector after 1935, federal employees were denied access to parallel arrangements for settling labor-management conflicts and had to rely upon political action to advance their goals. Operating in a unique labor market with entrance requirements, work rules, and job rights that differed from those prevailing in the private sector, the emerging federal unions were forced to "bargain" with Congress to achieve ends that private sector unions gained at the bargaining table.

In 1949 the Hoover Commission noted the frustration of public employees with their system, and recommended that they be given a greater say in setting their pay and working conditions.[1] In the belief that federal employees are entitled to be represented by officials of their own choosing as are their counterparts in the private sector, bills providing for formal recognition to civil service unions were introduced unsuccessfully in every session of Congress from 1949 to 1961. Although the successive postmaster generals, the comptroller generals, and members of the Civil Service Commission consistently opposed bargaining rights for federal workers and defeated these initiatives, the absence of formal bargaining rights did not halt the gradual growth of federal unions. Even though the new unions were forced to target their demands on politicians, 13 percent of all nonpostal federal employees were organized by 1961.

As a result of obstacles to organization, unions first took hold in those areas of federal employment most similar to the private sector. Postal workers had a strong sense of identity and were among the first to organize. Blue collar workers, benefiting from a greater acceptance of their organized activities, were also heavily unionized. In contrast, by 1961 organizing efforts had made few inroads among white collar civil servants; for example, a search of the State Department's employment rolls turned up only eleven white collar union members. Lacking legitimized organizational protection, white collar workers relied upon civil service rules for their protection rather than on collective action through organization.

The labor relations policies of federal agencies mirrored the union pattern of development. In general, the more similar the agency's function to one performed in the private sector, the more likely it was to have a developed labor relations program.[2] A 1961 survey revealed that twenty-one federal agencies discussed limited local issues with unions, eleven had only the "barest minimum" of dialogue, and another twenty-one had no policy toward unions at all. Thus, both membership levels and the nature of labor-management relations varied widely by occupation and agency.[3]

A Foothold for Unions

With the election of President Kennedy in 1960, the unions finally found a sympathetic ear in the White House. Early in his administration, Kennedy (at the urging of his secretary of labor, Arthur Goldberg) agreed to push for the adoption of legislation that would provide for limited collective bargaining rights in the federal government. When opposition in Congress prevented timely action on the administration's initiative, Kennedy secured the future of organized labor in the federal sector by acting unilaterally through an executive order.

The basic thrust of Executive Order 10988, issued in 1962, was to establish the right of federal employees to form and join unions. It provided for informal, formal, and exclusive recognition of federal unions, but stopped short of creating a system of collective bargaining and it limited the scope of bargaining even when it did occur. In addition, employee rights remained subordinated to agency action in the "public interest." Although the Kennedy order legitimized the existence of unions as participants in the federal employment system, it provided only a starting point for unions without assuring them significant leverage in promoting the interests of their members.

The administration's action was in part a response to the increasing membership in federal unions, but the executive order was itself a spur to union growth in representation and membership (Figure 1).[4] From 1963 to 1969 the number of federal employees represented by unions jumped from 180,000 to 843,000. Since 1972, such gains have slowed considerably, at least partially because the work force has to a great extent already been organized. By 1980, 86 percent of all blue collar Federal Wage System (FWS) employees and 54 percent of General Schedule (GS) white collar employees were covered by exclusive units. Overall, federal unions now represent 1.2 million employees, 61 percent of the total federal work force.

Actual union membership falls well below this level of representation among federal workers (Table 1). For example, only about one-third of the employees covered under contracts negotiated by the American Federation of Government Employees (AFGE) are members of the union. In some agencies the comparable ratio is only 8 to 10 percent. Aggregate estimates are that 30 to 35 percent of employees represented by unions pay membership dues, but reliable membership figures are difficult to come by.[5] Unions are not required to report federal membership, and no attempt is made to verify membership claims, although the number of paid members can be estimated from the financial statements which unions are required to report.

The substantial gap between levels of representation and membership in the federal sector has led critics to question whether the unions truly represent federal workers. The pattern evident in the private sector presents a stark contrast to the experience of federal unions. A study of private sector union coverage and membership found that, in 1976, 91 percent of workers represented by unions were also dues-paying members.[6] Still, as noted by Anthony Ingrassia, former head of labor-manage-

Figure 1. Union representation as a percentage of
the federal work force, 1963-1981

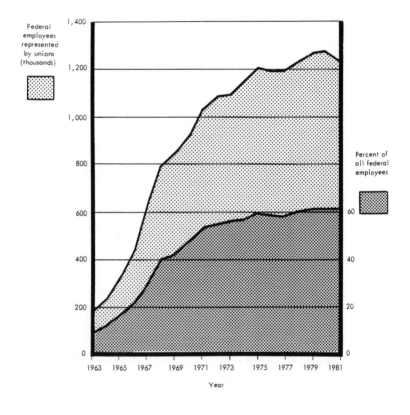

Source: Office of Personnel Management.

ment relations for the Office of Personnel Management, "union membership is lower in the federal sector, and this affects management's perception of the union as the representative of its employees."[7]

No doubt, the statutory prohibition against the agency shop in the
federal sector accounts in large part for the lagging union membership

16

Table 1. In 1981 four unions accounted for 81 percent of all federal workers represented by unions

Union	Affiliation	Estimated Membership*	Number Represented	Employees Represented per Dues Payer	Percent of Workforce Represented by Unions
American Federation of Government Employees	AFL-CIO	255,000	692,000	2.7	34
National Federation of Federal Employees	Independent	40,000	136,000	3.4	7
National Treasury Employee's Union	Independent	53,000	107,000	2.0	5
National Association of Government Employees	AFL-CIO	50,000	76,000	1.5	4
Metal Trades Council	AFL-CIO	N.A.	66,000	N.A.	3
International Association of Machinists	AFL-CIO	7,500	36,000	4.8	2
Other	—	N.A.	121,000	N.A.	6
Total	—	450,000	1,234,000	N.A.	61

Sources: Adapted from Office of Personnel Management, Union Representation in the Federal Government 1981 (Washington: Government Printing Office, November 1981); and Bureau of Labor Statistics preliminary 1981 union membership surveys.

*Membership figures used are self-reported by the unions to the Bureau of Labor Statistics, and there is no effort made to verify them. In 1982 NAGE joined the International Union of Service Employees, AFL-CIO.

in the federal government. Unionists contend that much of the disparity between representation and membership in the federal government stems from the unwillingness of the Congress to allow unions the security of agency shop fees, through which everyone would share the costs of securing common benefits. The Supreme Court has declared the "agency shop" or "union shop" constitutional, and such fair-share agreements (in which nonmembers must pay a fee equal to monthly dues) contribute to higher levels of membership in the private sector. Yet the Congress, perhaps concerned by the politicized nature of federal unions, has refused to permit what amounts to mandatory membership in federal unions.

The concept of an agency shop has repeatedly evoked concerns that union political activities may be incompatible with the beliefs of individual employees, and that compulsory payment of dues infringes upon the individual's freedom of association. Some opponents have gone so far as to suggest that the lack of union security created by the ban on agency shops forces federal unions to represent more carefully all employees in the unit. These arguments do not offer justification for the current distinction between public and private sectors with regard to agency shops, and ignore the difficulty in distinguishing between activity to further traditional union ends, and "purely political" practices. Furthermore, courts have approved plans whereby members choosing not to participate in political activity may be refunded that portion of their dues which would have been utilized for such purposes. Given the requirement that a union must negotiate for *all* employees in the unit, the current prohibition on agency shop fees precludes unions of federal employees from closing the gap between representation and membership in the federal work force.

Other federal-private sector comparisons are more favorable to unions of federal employees. In 1980 the bar against agency shops notwithstanding, only a slightly larger percentage of the total private sector work force paid dues to unions than did federal employees (20.9 percent versus 18.3 percent). While unionization in state and local governments surpassed that at the federal level in the mid-1960s, only 32 percent of all state and local employees are now covered by union agreements, compared to 57 percent of the federal work force. Because of the inclusion of retirees in membership statistics, it is difficult to tell what percentage of employees represented also pay dues at the state and local levels. Five states do have mandatory agency shop, however, and fifteen states, the Virgin Island territories, and the District of Columbia permit it.[8]

Thus, while federal unions have remained handicapped, they still have managed to obtain reasonable levels of support. The appeal of unions has varied considerably within the federal work force, and is a function of occupational roles and agency functions. The unions consist of a few large organizations and scores of affiliated and independent specialized unions, which serve relatively small segments of the federal work force. Representation is diverse. Even with a more established role in employee relations, federal unions seldom speak with a single voice.

Union Structure

In 1980 federal agencies had recognized 49 independent unions and 41 AFL-CIO affiliates. The nonaffiliated unions accounted for 29 percent

of union representation in the federal work force and the unions affiliated with the AFL-CIO represented the balance. The affiliated unions
have profited from the federation's greater resources for bargaining,
political activity, and organizing. They also have been more aggressive
in their organizing efforts, seizing upon the 1962 executive order in a
manner shunned by some nonaffiliated unions. For example, the American Federation of Government Employees (the largest affiliated union)
considered the 1962 executive order an "unparalleled opportunity,"
while the National Federation of Federal Employees (independent),
concerned that it would weaken lobbying functions, opposed the order.
Not until several years later, when the leadership of NFFE changed, did
that union begin actively recruiting new members.[9]

Although there are significant differences among federal unions, most
share certain characteristics. While locals of private sector unions retain
about 50 percent of dues, the local-national fund distribution in the
federal sector is closer to a 70-30 split. Locals thus have a secure financial
base.[10] The federal national unions tend to maintain lower reserves than
nationals in the private sector; with federal employee strikes illegal and
reasonably rare, the national need not maintain a strike fund. In 1982
monthly union dues averaged between $5.10 and $6.50.

A second common thread appears to be the predominance of women,
at least in the largest white collar unions. One union official characterized
federal employment as a young women's labor movement. Clerical and
other office employees are prime targets for current and future organization, and many of them are women. While there are important excep-
tions, much of the militancy of some federal unions is generated by
these members. A manifestation of this was shown during the 1980
AFGE election, at which both women and minority groups bolstered
their representation in policymaking and increased sensitivity to their
needs in collective bargaining.[11]

A third common characteristic of federal unions is their pursuit of
aggressive consolidation policies. The structure of federal bargaining as
well as of the unions is becoming more centralized. As unions reorganize on an agency-wide basis (rather than regionally), through consolidation of intra-agency locals, and labor relations functions gradually
concentrate at headquarters, the focus of bargaining is shifting to increased emphasis on agency levels. This centralization carries advantages
for both sides. Some federal managers find national agreements administratively convenient, while unions gain enhanced bargaining scope

in that agency rules cannot be invoked as a potential obstacle in negotiations. There are disadvantages as well. While consolidated unions may be able to force more concessions from management, the local supplements may be costly to administer. Their leadership may also become less responsive to membership wishes as it becomes increasingly difficult to marshal the greater resources needed to challenge and unseat incumbents. Yet on balance most unions have seen centralization as a positive development and pushed for further consolidation of the fragmented federal union structure.

The Big Four and the Little Ones

Beyond these common attributes, and notwithstanding their frequently shared goals and tactics, the individual federal unions each have their own unique structure and priorities. By far the largest single union is the American Federation of Government Employees (AFGE), an AFL-CIO affiliate, followed by another AFL-CIO affiliate and two white collar independents. A review of the history and structure of the four largest federal unions and two blue collar AFL-CIO affiliates provides a useful sketch of the role of organized labor in contemporary federal employee relations (Figure 2).

American Federation of Government Employees (AFGE)

AFGE has become the biggest and most politically powerful federal union (postal work force excluded), representing over half of all employees who are covered by exclusively recognized units. AFGE was chartered by the American Federation of Labor in 1932 after the National Federation of Federal Employees left the federation to become an independent union.

The 255,000 members claimed by AFGE (the 1982 convention indicated a dues-paying membership of 225,000) accounted for almost one of every twelve full-time federal employees and constituted 37 percent of all employees represented by AFGE. The largest segment of the membership is composed of clerical workers (45 percent), with blue collar workers accounting for 40 percent and professionals for 15 percent of AFGE members. Since blue collar workers total only 27 percent of employees represented by the union but make up 40 percent of its dues payers, it seems they have a greater propensity to join the union that serves them. This is borne out by the experience of the other major

Figure 2. Unions represent about 1.25 million federal employees

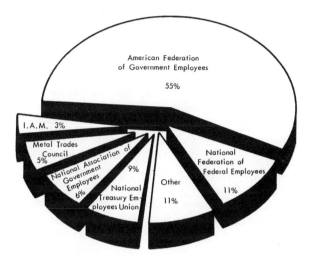

American Federation
of Government Employees

55%

I.A.M. 3%

Metal Trades
Council
5%

National Association of
Government
Employees
6%

9%

National
Treasury Em-
ployees Union

Other

11%

National
Federation of
Federal Employees

11%

Source: Office of Personnel Management and Bureau of Labor Statistics.

federal unions. Those represented by the union are organized into approximately 1,250 locals. Members pay a basic $5.10 per month in dues, but each local may assess higher dues. The 1982 convention defeated a proposal to boost the monthly dues by $1.35.

Originally the union was structured along the same lines as the agencies with which it dealt. Locals organized along geographic lines coincided with the management organization, creating a structure that encouraged the proliferation of rules and regulations under the 1962 executive order. Today, both sides have altered the way they do business. AFGE is carrying out an internal reorganization that will consolidate locals within the same agency, while federal agencies have centralized their labor-management relations functions. Union locals, especially larger ones such as that in the Social Security Administration, are gaining greater autonomy over their own affairs, while the national headquarters is evolving into a central education, research, and lobbying body. This is not to say that AFGE has lost control over its locals—the national still steps in when problems occur. Indeed, some have argued that the growth of national units has tended to centralize power in national union headquarters.

Because of its size and its affiliation with the AFL-CIO, AFGE enjoys unique political clout. When President Carter proposed his civil service reforms, he consulted with the AFL-CIO and the AFGE leadership to a much greater extent than with any other union. Kenneth T. Blaylock, president of the AFGE, explained that the administration "came to us because George Meany told President Carter that if he wanted the federation's support, he should get together with AFGE."[12] Carter followed this advice, and both AFGE and the AFL-CIO wound up supporting the reform legislation while the three major independent unions opposed it.

The dominant influence of AFGE is exhibited in numerous ways. Its political action committee (which changed its name to AFGE-PAC for the 1982 elections) raised $249,000 to support candidates for federal offices in the 1980 elections. The union anticipated raising a higher amount in 1982, mostly to support Democratic candidates. In addition to the promotion of its interests on Capitol Hill, AFGE has a central role in the administrative machinery of the pay-setting process. Its representative, George Hobt, has emerged as the informal spokesman for the other unions, particularly for those within the federation, on matters relating to the blue collar pay system.

The size of the union, however, has proven to be a mixed blessing. Because of the diversity of interests it represents, centrifugal forces occasionally threaten to pull AFGE apart. Internal strife nearly led to the ouster of incumbent president Kenneth T. Blaylock, who barely defeated his challenger by a tally of 109,414 to 107,052 during the 1978 union convention. At that time, the delegates also rebuked union officials for their support of Carter's reform legislation. Similarly, in 1980 Carl Sadler, former legislative director of the union, lost to Blaylock in a contested election. The results were investigated by the U.S. Department of Labor, which found some of the complaints justified but decided it was too late to rerun the election. By 1982, Blaylock gained wider support of the membership beating Sadler decisively by a 120,529 to 48,127 vote.

The variety of interests that the union must represent contributes to AFGE's difficulties in other ways as well. The voices of both blue collar and white collar members must be heeded, yet they are occasionally at odds with one another. There are a great many locals and a limited number of national representatives to service them, leading to an over-reliance on local leaders with varying experience and ability. Dissatisfaction with this kind of arrangement caused delegates at recent AFGE conventions to demand greater responsiveness from the national headquarters.[13] Finally, some members have charged that AFL-CIO affiliation conflicts with members' concerns, occasionally forcing AFGE leaders to sacrifice the interest of their organization in order to retain standing in the federation. For example, a strong stand against contracting out might conflict with private sector unions affiliated with the AFL-CIO.

Despite its internal discords, AFGE remains the predominant federal union. And while certain groups with a high degree of group identification (such as IRS employees) will no doubt cling to their own unions, the official AFGE line is that over time the union will absorb most other federal employee organizations.

National Federation of Federal Employees (NFFE)

Next to AFGE, the second largest federal union is the independent National Federation of Federal Employees (NFFE). Established as an AFL affiliate in 1917, the union quit the federation fourteen years later because it felt its role as a lobbying agent was hampered by the more traditional union activity. This action was decisive in molding the character of the union over the next half century.

NFFE now represents 136,000 workers, mostly clerical and professional, who are organized into some 400 locals. Approximately 30 percent of those represented paid in 1981 the monthly $5.50 in dues. According to union estimates, about 40 percent of its members are blue collar workers who comprise only 22 percent of all those represented, indicating again that federal blue collar employees appear to join their union at a greater rate than other employees.

The management of locals in NFFE resembles that found in AFGE.

The national headquarters services the bargaining of locals, but devotes the bulk of its resources, including the time of about seventy staffers, to research, education, and political action. This approach is common in unions whose membership is split between blue and white collar segments. While tension between the two is not a major problem, each requires different types of service that are best provided through a less coordinated structure. The diversity of interests is illustrated by an anecdote told by one NFFE staff member about the 1981 Professional Air Traffic Controllers Organization strike. When news of the PATCO action became known, phone calls from their own members flooded NFFE headquarters. The blue collar unionists demanded to know when their sympathy walkout was to begin; the white collar people were, for the most part, adamant that NFFE not get involved in any job action.

As the largest of forty-nine independent unions representing federal workers in 1980, NFFE presumably could have a powerful role in shaping the direction of organized labor in the federal sector. Indeed, smaller unions that represent workers in a single agency (i.e., Patent Office Professional Union) or unions that organized workers in a particular skill or craft (International Federation of Federal Police; Association of Civilian Technicians) generally rely on their larger independent brothers for leadership. Yet NFFE's membership has been declining steadily in recent years, and its political action committee collected and spent only $47,000 in support of 55 federal candidates in the 1980 elections. With its sizable base of dues-paying members, NFFE still has the resources to support a level of information and political activity that smaller independents cannot afford. The union has not taken, however, the aggressive action necessary to lead the smaller like-minded unions, leading one unfriendly observer to charge that the most significant activity of the NFFE is to act as an insurance agent for its members.

National Treasury Employees' Union (NTEU)

The aggressive and militant role shirked by NFFE has been embraced by the second largest independent union, the National Treasury Employees Union. NTEU was first established in 1938 as a fraternal organization of Internal Revenue Service collectors. When that agency was restructured in the 1950s, the union expanded its jurisdiction to include all IRS employees and by 1973 it represented over 90 percent of both the IRS and the Bureau of Alcohol, Tobacco, and Firearms. In 1973 the union assumed its present name and broadened its jurisdiction to all Treasury Department employees, and has since actively recruited employees in several other agencies. NTEU currently represents over 100,000 employees, more than half of whom are members. In many units membership runs 70-75 percent, giving NTEU by far the highest membership/representation ratio of the major federal unions.

NTEU's relationship with its local units eschews the looser approach pursued by AFGE and NFFE, emphasizing instead a more aggressive and centralized bargaining strategy. The large and activist eighty-two-person national headquarters staff maintains close ties with NTEU's approximately 225 locals, assists them in their bargaining and represents NTEU members in grievance and arbitration hearings. Unlike some of the other major federal unions, NTEU is extensively involved in determining which grievance and arbitration cases from its locals reach the Federal Labor Relations Authority or arbitrators, enabling the union continually to press forward new issues that more clearly delineate the scope of bargaining rights. As in the landmark *Bureau of Public Debt* case in which the union unsuccessfully challenged management's right to set performance standards, NTEU provides highly planned and professional representation in traditionally local grievance and arbitration matters as a means of promoting the interests of the broader membership.[14]

NTEU's reputation as an aggressive and effective union is not solely based on its bargaining activities, although it is often rated at the top of the list in that respect. NTEU has been active in pursuing its cause through the courts as well. Its most notable success story stemmed from President Nixon's attempt to delay the statutory federal pay adjustment deadline during his imposed freeze on wages and prices. NTEU challenged the presidential action, taking the case all the way to the U.S. Supreme Court, and won. The result was probably the largest back pay award in history, totaling over $600 million.[15] The union's successful fight against the ban on picketing was another of many examples of its persistence and its effectiveness in defending and advancing the rights of federal workers.[16]

The strident political activities of NTEU also illustrate its militancy. Considered by some congressional and other sources as the most effective lobbyist for federal employees, the union is continuing to beef up its political arm.[17] For the 1980 elections, the Treasury Employees' Political Action Committee (TEPAC) raised $173,000 and spent nearly $149,000 in support of 114 candidates for federal office.

NTEU values its independence from the AFL-CIO, indicating no desire to join AFGE as a part of the federation. On the contrary, NTEU was among the three large independents that pushed for bargaining over wages in 1978 when AFGE had already committed itself to support a civil service reform bill without such provisions. There is no indication that NTEU will abandon in the foreseeable future its highly independent and vocal posture in favor of any advantage that affiliation or merger might offer.

National Association of Government Employees (NAGE)

Founded in 1947, the National Association of Government Employees represents 76,000 federal workers, making it the fourth largest federal union in terms of representation. (It does not publish membership statistics.) About 60 percent of its estimated membership are blue collar workers, a larger proportion of blue collar workers than in the other big three unions. NAGE also acts as a "mini federation" by including two federal union affiliates, the International Brotherhood of Police Officers (IBPO) and the Federal Aviation Science and Technology Association (FASTA). In 1982 NAGE affiliated with the AFL-CIO.

A relatively small proportion of NAGE members are in the federal government. Most of the union's strength lies in state and local governments, coloring the union's priorities and programs. Like AFGE, NAGE holds little sway over the actions of its federal sector locals in bargaining activities. The political operation of NAGE is much less sophisticated on the federal level than that of its rivals, and it has no PAC to help elect friendly federal officials. In 1978 NAGE joined the other two large independent unions in opposing the civil service reform bill because it made no provision for wage negotiations.

Other Employee Representatives

The "big four" unions represent a substantial portion of the work force, but the story does not end with them. As noted earlier, there are over eighty other affiliated and independent unions. In addition, some federal blue collar workers are represented by unions whose membership is predominantly in the private sector. Blue collar unions with significant portions of the federal work force include the International Association of Machinists (IAM), the Service Employees International Union (SEIU), and the International Brotherhood of Electrical Workers (IBEW).[18]

The blue collar unions focus most of their attention on the pay process, which is used as a "back door" for bargaining over wages. To implement the concept of wage comparability, union representatives participate with management in decisions such as number of firms and job classifications to be surveyed. Since the stakes for the unions are high, local union officials invest a great deal of time and effort to ensure quality input to advance the interests of their members. In the past the results of these surveys were crucial in setting local wage levels of federal blue collar employees. Since 1979, however, when blue collar pay was tied to that of white collar workers through across-the-board limitations on both, political action has become more important to the livelihood of federal blue collar workers, and their unions have increased their lobbying efforts and taken a greater interest in agency budgets. Locals of blue collar federal employees are part of private sector unions and their contributions for political activities are funneled through the unions' central political apparatus, either its own political action committee, or that of the AFL-CIO.

A number of blue collar unions belong to the public employee department (PED) of the AFL-CIO, although with the exception of the AFGE only a small percentage of each union is made up of federal employees. The PED has a separate staff which assists member unions in political, administrative, and bargaining matters and offers expertise often not available within individual unions. The department provides these diverse services, including research, assistance in negotiations, and coordination of political activity, for a per capita tax of between three and four cents per member per month. This is in addition to an AFL-CIO per capita monthly nineteen-cent assessment for all affiliated unions.

Another general association is the Metal Trades Council (MTC), whose membership includes some unions with federal employees in their ranks and some locals directly affiliated with AFL-CIO unions. For a minimum of fifty cents per member per month, the MTC services unions by providing bargaining and political advice. Two of its largest members are the International Association of Machinists and the International Brotherhood of Electrical Workers.

Participation in the pay determination process, membership in the AFL-CIO, and the somewhat lesser degree of participation in political activity all contribute to the image of blue collar unions as more closely resembling private sector unions than other unions of federal employees. However, their limited scope of bargaining and the fact that wage "negotiations" are still carried on in the political arena distinguish the federal locals from their private sector counterparts.

White collar unions tend to be small independents based on a narrow occupational group or in a single agency. Some are quite powerful within their departments: the Professional Air Traffic Controllers Organization (PATCO) was the outstanding example. These smaller unions tend to focus on their own special interests in negotiations, although some maintain active lobbying arms which concentrate on pay battles on Capitol Hill.

Why Unions for Federal Workers?

In light of the limited scope of bargaining in the federal sector, it is not self-evident why federal workers join and support unions. The facile explanation that joining a union is an act of defiance fails to explain how unions retain sustained membership support and even growth. Clearly some two of every ten federal employees who pay their dues believe that the union is worth the price and six of every ten have expressed an interest in being represented by unions.

Certainly some workers choose to join federal unions for the protection of employee rights and for the improvement in working conditions. Unions in the federal establishment are gaining experience and sophistication in the collective bargaining game. Complaints regularly voiced following the 1962 executive order about amateurism and lack of experience at the bargaining table are heard less often. The bargaining process has become more important, and the parties have come to know each other better. As one union leader observed: "The negotiations process is a very personal affair. You begin to know your adversaries. You understand their sensitivities, their level of dedication, and above all their level of sophistication."[19]

It appears that every step toward greater effectiveness at the bargaining table brings more believers into the fold of federal unions. Activity escalates in proportion to the perceived cumulative grievances and the ability to translate activism into tangible results. The meager pay increases since the mid-1970s have raised prospects for union growth. The blows to job security administered by the Reagan administration are also likely to strengthen the appeal of unions to the federal labor force.

Furthermore, it seems that the limitations on collective bargaining strengthen perceptions of the importance of unions among federal workers. Because so many issues are excluded from negotiations, federal employees need a political organization that will represent their interests by attempting to influence federal decision makers. While there is a demonstrated willingness on the part of federal unions to work within the established framework of lobbying and collective bargaining, they will pursue this course only so long as legitimate solutions can be achieved. When nothing more can be gained at the negotiation table, the only alternative to resignation is a militant and politicized labor movement.

Federal employee unions, of course, are not the only ones that turn to political lobbying as a means for furthering worker interests. Given the federal government's pervasive involvement in many aspects of the economy, unions bargaining with private employers find it increasingly necessary to make extensive forays to Capitol Hill. For example, the United Auto Workers found recently that the livelihood of a significant portion of its membership depended upon federal government policies to aid a faltering automobile company. Just as construction unions lobby the Labor Department on the definition of "prevailing wage" in the Davis-Bacon Act, so do the unions representing federal employees become involved in the comparability machinery that determines federal pay.

Yet the federal unions rely more heavily on political processes than their private sector counterparts, partly because of the restrictions on collective bargaining rights in the federal sector and partly because the Congress frequently plays the role of management's "board of directors" in setting federal employee policies. As long as the bread and butter issues of federal compensation are kept off the bargaining table, federal unions will have little choice but to emphasize lobbying tactics in their efforts to represent their members.

3

The Emergence of Collective Bargaining

In their pursuit of bargaining rights for federal workers, federal unions have provided the driving force behind the gradual expansion of issues that can be brought to the negotiating table. Conversely, the very development of collective bargaining institutions enhanced the standing of federal unions by creating formal channels of communication between labor representatives and management.

The executive order issued by President Kennedy in 1962 (E.O. 10988) afforded the first breakthrough in the emergence of collective bargaining. It provided official sanction for federal unions and a recognition that at least some labor-management issues should be resolved at the negotiating table. It was a significant victory for organized labor in the federal sector, and it gave an impetus for the expansion of negotiating rights which continues to this day.

Adjustments and Modifications

The past two decades have been characterized by marginal but nearly constant change within the federal collective bargaining system. In the years immediately following the Kennedy order, the growth in union membership accentuated the shortcomings of the executive order's attempt to decentralize management authority. The lack of a centralized administrative structure resulted in a plethora of rules and regulations unique to each agency and without any semblance of coordination or consistency. The disadvantages of this fragmented structure gradually came to outweigh any benefits of increased flexibility as unions proliferated, so that by the late 1960s most observers acknowledged a need for a more uniform management approach to collective bargaining.

To study these concerns and recommend remedial steps, President Johnson established a labor-management relations review committee. Its report was not officially submitted, and President Nixon reconstituted a similar study committee which recognized the discontents of organized labor and federal managers, but emphasized "the need, above all, in public service to preserve the public interest as the paramount consideration."[1] Any dramatic change in the emerging collective bargaining system would have proven highly controversial, particularly because most federal managers still perceived union advances as detrimental to the efficient operation of the government. Apparently they viewed themselves as capable of serving the public interest and providing for employee welfare without intervention by unions. Thus, it was hardly surprising that the study committee proposed only modest adjustments to the existing bargaining system, emphasizing a more coherent policy of administration among federal agencies.

The basic thrust of the committee's recommendations was incorporated by President Nixon in his 1969 Executive Order 11491. The order made no significant additions to bargaining rights, but instead sought to provide a centralized structure though which top Federal management could coordinate and administer the collective bargaining process. In attempting to halt the proliferation of disparate agency rules and to establish a mechanism for resolving labor-management disputes, E.O. 11491 established the Federal Labor Relations Council (FLRC), consisting of the chairman of the Civil Service Commission, the secretary of labor, and the director of the Bureau of the Budget (later the Office of Management and Budget). The council was charged with the responsibility for the general administration of the program, hearing appeals, and issuing regulations, while the Department of Labor's assistant secretary for labor-management relations was to administer daily operations.

Although the 1969 order strengthened the institutional backing for dealing with the marginal issues within the scope of collective bargaining, it left most aspects of federal employee relations to unilateral management discretion. Wage and fringe benefit determination continued to be the exclusive domain of the Congress, allowing only narrow adminis-

31

trative personnel issues to be addressed directly through collective bargaining. The Nixon executive order did place limits on capricious actions by management, denying agency heads the power to veto union agreements except when they did not conform to laws, rules, and regulations, but the steps toward a neutral structure for labor-management relations in the federal sector were small at best.

Responding to pressures for change from the unions, President Nixon issued in the following six years three more executive orders (E.O. 11616, 11636, and 11838). These orders broadened slightly the scope of bargaining and increased the number of grievances that could be covered by a negotiated procedure, but they established few new employee rights. Instead, the orders tended to identify the needs of agency management with the dictates of the public interest. This presumed link justified the unwillingness of the Congress and the executive branch to share their powers with employees or their unions.

While these periodic modifications of the collective bargaining system addressed management concerns for efficient administration in federal employee relations, they failed to deal with labor's aspirations to eliminate the severe constraints on negotiability imposed by the Kennedy and Nixon orders and to broaden the scope of collective bargaining. For more than a decade and a half following Kennedy's 1962 executive order, the parameters for bargaining in the federal sector remained virtually unchanged, broadened only modestly by court rulings resulting from union challenges to interpretations of those limitations. Given the discontent of federal unions with this lack of progress, there is less reason to question why the Congress adopted legislation concerning collective bargaining in 1978 than to wonder why the debate did not occur sooner.

There are several explanations for the inaction of Congress with regard to collective bargaining in the federal sector. Successive presidents have never viewed the right of federal employees to bargain collectively as a high priority, and President Kennedy's circumvention of the Congress through his executive order may have placed the issue squarely in the chief executive's domain. More convincingly, federal unions may not have had sufficient political clout to persuade the Congress to act on collective bargaining statutes. In the absence of such overwhelming pressure, the Congress may have been content to avoid conflict over divisive issues of employee rights and management prerogatives. Whatever the reason, when Congress lost the initative to Kennedy in 1962, sixteen years elapsed until Congress became an active partner in enacting legislation affecting labor-management relations in the federal government.

An Attempt at Legislative Reforms

By 1978 there seemed to be a consensus that an overhauling of labor-management rules was in order. At one extreme, unions favored expanding the scope of collective bargaining to parallel private industry practices. From the opposite perspective, federal managers insisted that "the whole system militates against effective organization."[2] The managers argued that the existing statutory protection for workers against management action should be more than enough to satisfy the unions, and that existing rules and regulations already were hampering the efficiency of government. Thus, while the need for change was broadly recognized, there was no understanding between labor and management as to the remedies that should be applied.

The initial stages in the development of a civil service reform proposal ignored employee concerns. As formulated by the Carter administration, improved efficiency in government served as the prime objective and orientation of its efforts. President Carter began his reform initiatives in 1977 by seeking broad authority to reorganize federal agencies, viewing this action as a means of trimming the size of the bureaucracy and making it more responsive to public needs. This authority, first established in 1949, had lapsed in 1973. Always eager to strike a blow at bureaucracy Congress restored these executive powers four years later (Public Law 95-17).[3] Carter made immediate use of this option, beginning two executive branch reorganizations in 1977 and implementing another four in 1978.

While pursuing the search for a more responsive federal bureaucracy through reorganization, President Carter appointed a task force of 120 federal personnel management experts to recommend changes in the civil service that would bring about greater efficiency and flexibility in its operations. Unions were not persuaded by President Carter's argument that reform was in the interests of employees as well as management, particularly since their representatives were not even invited to participate in the task force, although their views were periodically sought. While Carter developed an administration proposal, the unions continued to insist that collective bargaining was the only acceptable means of reforming the system, and sympathetic members of the House Post Office and Civil Service Committee introduced bills that would have extended the scope of collective bargaining to a broad range of subjects, including pay.

The clash of interests between unions and managers was to a large extent inevitable. In an effort to forestall union opposition to his legislation, President Carter promised that he would pursue the twin objectives of reorganization and protection of employee rights, and that no employee would be fired or demoted as a result of the reform. Needless to say, this pledge evoked as much skepticism as reassurance. Raymond Jacobson, executive director of the Civil Service Commission, wrote to the OMB expressing "deep concern" that the antithetical positions could not successfully be reconciled.[4]

Notwithstanding such pledges of good will, the administration did seek to avoid issues of collective bargaining pushed by federal unions. Only when it became clear that civil service reform legislation would not move out of committee without some response to union concerns did President Carter agree to include provisions that expanded bargaining rights and access to arbitration procedures. It is difficult to ascertain the extent to which the administration had planned to make the concessions. Some observers believe that Carter established a "bargaining position" by ignoring labor's concerns and then struck a calculated "compromise" which fell far short of union demands for full-scale bargaining and the right to strike. Others contend that the designers of the legislation recognized belatedly the need to defuse union opposition, and therefore acquiesced to the addition of the new Title VII that addressed collective bargaining rights. In either case, the last-minute bargaining amendments mollified the American Federation of Government Employees, the largest union of government employees, and more importantly removed AFL-CIO opposition to passage of the administration's reform initiative.

Not all unions joined the fray on the side of the administration. Some—notably the National Treasury Employees Union—opposed the tame labor relations provisions, arguing that to settle for a weak program would hurt chances of ever obtaining more comprehensive bargaining rights. In addition, some managers felt that the administration had compromised its original goal of making the civil service more flexible and responsive to direction from above by extending protections for federal employees. It is likely, however, that less balanced legislation, in either direction, would have failed to secure the broad support in Congress necessary for its passage.

The Civil Service Reform Act of 1978 (P.L. 95-454) was signed into law on October 13, 1978. Many of the initiatives favored in the original bill had been watered down, and some provisions were added, including the maintenance of some veterans' preference provisions (which Carter wanted to eliminate) and Title VII, the section on labor-management relations. In its final form, the legislation:

1. Enacted merit principles into law for the first time.

2. Split the Civil Service Commission into the Office of Personnel Management (OPM) and the Merit Systems Protection Board (MSPB). The latter was to rule on employee appeals from management actions.

3. Mandated a system of performance evaluations to be set up by the agencies and OPM. Personnel actions based on performance ratings were to be subject to review and appeal, and unfavorable evaluations had to be expunged from files if performance improved.

4. Ended the five-point preference for nondisabled retired veterans at or above the rank of major or lieutenant commander. Veterans with 30 percent or more disability were to be entitled to a review of agency denials of employment from civil service registers.

5. Set up a Senior Executive Service (SES), composed of top-level employees who chose to trade off some employment security for a chance at promised opportunities for greater financial reward. Mid-level management salary boosts also became contingent upon performance.

6. Established the Federal Labor Relations Authority (FLRA) as the administrator of the labor relations programs, similar to the National Labor Relations Board in the private sector. Most provisions of the 1969 executive order were incorporated into law, with a slight increase in the scope of bargaining and arbitration rights.

The administration tried to sell its proposed overhaul of the civil service as a thoroughgoing reform, but the final legislation adopted by Congress left most aspects of federal employee relations unchanged. Through its control over the purse strings, Congress still dictates the level of pay and fringe benefits, and the Civil Service Reform Act did not alter federal salary structures or the methods by which wages were set and positions classified. Congress also rejected an expanded union role by refusing to grant further collective bargaining rights over wages and fringe benefits. Even the issue of union security was left untouched by the reform bill, and federal unions are still denied the right to collect agency shop fees from the employees they represent.

The Civil Service Reform Act did alter the structure of federal labor-management relations in some significant ways. First, with the creation of the Federal Labor Relations Authority to serve as arbiter, the interpretation and administration of the law were placed in neutral hands. The old management-dominated council had never been able to convince federal unions of its impartiality, and the creation of a panel of labor relations experts who had no vested management interests helped to increase the legitimacy of the new law in the eyes of many federal unions. Second, all grievance procedures initiated by federal employees under negotiated contracts now must have arbitration as their final step. This greater reliance on arbitration was applied, however, to a narrow set of issues. Excluded from the expanded definition of grievances were pay and fringe benefits, position classification, discharge (handled by the Merit Systems Protection Board), Hatch Act violations, and entrance examinations. Third, and perhaps most importantly, the legislation opened significant "loopholes" in restrictions on negotiability which have enabled unions to broaden the scope of collective bargaining in the federal government.

Union Efforts to Broaden Negotiability

The sharp restrictions that the law places on the scope of collective bargaining have caused detractors to scoff at the intense battles waged over what they perceive as little more than bargaining over parking spaces and employee uniforms. Yet in practice federal unions have been able to push some additional items onto the bargaining table by seeking rigid adherence to provisions of the law that tend to restrict management prerogatives.

One of the statutory "loopholes" that federal unions have exploited, though sparingly, in their efforts to expand the scope of negotiability is the concept of "compelling need," initially introduced in 1975 as an amendment to Executive Order 11491. In general, only government-wide rules or laws can prevent bargaining over union proposals that are otherwise negotiable. However, the law allows an agency to refuse to bargain on proposals that are contrary to one of its own rules if there is compelling need not to infringe upon that rule. The FLRA has established four criteria for determining when a federal agency may legitimately invoke the compelling need rule: (1) it must be essential, as opposed to helpful or desirable, to the completion of an agency's mission or its management; (2) it must implement a mandate of law or a rule promulgated by higher authority; (3) it must be necessary to the maintenance of merit principles; or (4) it must establish uniformity on all or a substantial part of the agency where that is essential to the public interest.[5] If an agency rule meets one or more of these tests, the agency is not required by law to bargain over anything that would alter it, and the FLRA in turn would not overturn such a decision.

Section 7117(a)(3) of the Civil Service Reform Act includes one important exception to this rule. The agency may use the compelling need argument "unless an exclusive representative represents an appropriate unit including not less than a majority of the employees of the issuing agency or primary national subdivision, as the case may be, to whom the rule or regulation is applicable." The basic intent of this provision seems to have been to widen the scope of bargaining. A leading participant in drafting the law remarked that this provision was included "with the understanding that . . . the compelling need test will be permitted to be raised in only a limited number of cases."[6]

The Federal Labor Relations Authority has adhered to this strict interpretation in its decisions implementing the concept of compelling need. It has, for instance, found that a policy already implemented may be negotiable, even if costly to modify. Hence cost alone is not enough to bar negotiation.[7] The authority has also decided that union proposals must clearly interfere with the rule being defended if they are to be found non-negotiable.[8]

Before 1978, the agency head's interpretation was final and binding as to whether a union demand was negotiable. Thus a valid defense of non-negotiability on the part of the agency would have been to trot out the applicable rule and declare that it was consistent with the agency's position. Under the 1978 reform act, there is no similar presumption that the agency has the final word. Section 7105(i) permits the FLRA to seek an advisory opinion from the agency, but the law neither requires the authority to do so nor binds it to the agency view. The intervention of the FLRA as a neutral third party has thus been crucial to union efforts to limit the use of the "compelling need" provision and to broaden the scope of bargaining.

The second major basis used by unions of federal employees to broaden negotiability is derived from the right to negotiate over agency procedures to be followed in implementing decisions. The management rights clause (Section 7106) mandates negotiation over "procedures which management officials of the agency will observe in exercising any authority under this section." In practice, of course, the distinctions between procedural and substantive management actions are extremely difficult to discern. Federal unions still may not negotiate procedures that go to the heart of management rights, and the Federal Labor Relations Authority in some instances has ruled that union proposals which "directly interfere" with a manager's duties are non-negotiable. Yet the broader consequence of the Civil Service Reform Act provisions has been to give unions the leverage to negotiate over most management actions.

The management rights clause also requires that an agency, upon union demand, negotiate over the impact of its actions on employee working conditions. Management retains the right to act, but the ramifications of its decisions are subject to challenge by unions. Under the Nixon executive order, the Federal Labor Relations Council adopted a standard of "unreasonable delay" which precluded union proposals from significantly hampering the exercise of management's authority. The FLRA ruled, however, that proposals involving impact are negotiable unless they prevent management from "acting at all," a much more stringent standard than had been used in the past. This change brought loud complaints from federal agencies, which attempted to preserve management prerogatives by taking their case to court. The court deferred to the decision of the authority and rejected management's claim that "acting at all" would stop the gears of government.[9] Although the distinction between cases where "acting at all" and "direct interference" standards apply is necessarily muddy, a court has upheld the right of the FLRA to draw the line. As a result, the use of both "procedures" and "impact" bargaining can become significant tools for enlarging the scope of bargaining.

The 1978 reform legislation placed the FLRA squarely in the midst of negotiability disputes. With respect to work assignments, for example, the authority ruled that unions may negotiate over proposals preventing management from requiring employees, unless there is a clear operating need to do so, to travel on assignments where they would incur more than the allowable per diem.[10] The authority has also found negotiable proposals that would set criteria for deciding which applications for work outside the agency would be approved,[11] and which set procedures for defining the initial "area of consideration" for promotions (thus defining eligible candidates for first consideration).[12] In a case involving the "acting at all" standard, the union won the right to negotiate delay of a formal suspension until the review and appeals processes had been completely exhausted.[13] Finally, federal unions won the right to negotiate grievance procedures covering complaints about the fairness and equity of performance appraisals.[14]

Not all FLRA rulings on negotiability have served to broaden the scope of collective bargaining in the federal sector. An attempt by a union to force management to rotate assignments on the basis of seniority was rejected by the FLRA because it held that the union challenge constituted direct interference.[15] The authority has also rendered two landmark rulings which established that the determination of performance evaluation standards and the designation of a position's "critical elements" under provisions of the Civil Service Reform Act are solely management prerogatives insofar as they are "fair and equitable."[16] Attempts to negotiate the choice of these critical elements have been rebuffed by the FLRA.[17]

Four years after the passage of the CSRA it is still difficult to assess the extent to which FLRA rulings will expand the scope of negotiability in the federal establishment. The relatively small number of cases involving "procedure" and "impact" bargaining, as well as the vagueness of some FLRA decisions, is part of the problem. Striving for consensus, the FLRA members resorted too frequently to vague language and thus they failed to provide clear guidelines to management and labor as to the scope of negotiability. The impact of FLRA decisions will also depend on the composition of the authority's membership and on whether the unions have the resources and the will to present grievances. Clearly the law, as interpreted, allows unions to defer implementation of actions they oppose, although they cannot do so forever. Whether they will also become the basis for future inroads by federal unions into the realm of management rights will depend on the philosophical bent of the FLRA.

Apart from impact and procedures bargaining, neither the CSRA nor the interpretations of the FLRA have significantly expanded the scope of negotiations. One study regards earlier council and authority decisions as more or less congruent despite the changes adopted in the reform legislation.[18] Assignment of work, compensation, promotions, and other major personnel actions remain within the prerogative of management.

No doubt federal unions will continue efforts to chip away at restrictions on collective bargaining while management interests will seek to preserve or enhance their flexibility and discretion in the name of efficient government. It is on the balance between management prerogatives and worker rights that both the rationality and the integrity of federal employee relations rests.

Bargaining versus Management Rights

In the private sector, the National Labor Relations Board has tended over nearly five decades to expand the scope of issues subject to collective bargaining, leaving few personnel practices outside the pale of negotiability. The NLRB has taken its direction from the broad requirement spelled out in section 7(d) of the National Labor Relations Act: "To bargain collectively is the performance of the mutual obligation of the employer and the representative of the employees to meet at reasonable times and confer in good faith with respect to wages, hours, and other terms and conditions of employment." Negotiated agreements in the private sector normally incorporate a "management rights" clause which spells out management prerogatives but those rights are determined at the bargaining table.

Workers in the federal sector have no such influence over management rights because the law limits the scope of negotiations. Some members of Congress have continued to push for an expanded reliance on collective bargaining, arguing that "(f)ull discussions and negotiations will help keep management 'on its toes' and force it to reexamine its policies and procedures."[19] To date, however, the scope of bargaining remains severely limited.

A most provocative issue in federal employee relations is whether the balance between collective bargaining and management rights can be explained or justified in terms of the unique federal structure. Negotiability determinations have always sought to balance the concern for "efficiency in government" with that of the union right to a voice in certain decisions, but somehow efficiency in the federal sector has become inextricably linked to management rights. In contrast the federal law regulating collective bargaining in the private sector has affirmed the rights of workers to bargain over key aspects of their employment, and viewed an orderly system of collective bargaining which avoids sharp confrontations between management and labor as consistent with goals of overall efficiency. Similar arguments for negotiated resolutions of labor disputes could be readily applied to federal employment practices, yet policymakers repeatedly portray collective bargaining rights as the antithesis of efficiency in government, an unacceptable infringement of essential management prerogatives.

The distinctions drawn between private and federal employment are vividly illustrated in the ban on strikes by federal workers. While strikes by federal employees are rare, they have consistently been viewed as threats to the general welfare and as illegal acts of defiance. In 1937 President Roosevelt called strikes by federal workers "nothing less than an attempt . . . to prevent or obstruct the operations of government until their demands are satisfied. Such actions looking toward the paralysis of government by those who have sworn to uphold it are unthinkable and intolerable."[20] This argument was repeated by President Reagan in 1981 when he discharged the striking air traffic controllers. Opposition to strikes by federal workers generally revolves around perceived differences between public and private sectors.

The prohibition against federal strikes is most often defended as a necessary step for the protection of public health and safety. Many public employees—including fire, police, other law enforcement and emergency personnel—fulfill vital service roles, and their absence could cause significant damage to the public weal. Work stoppages by less visible employees could also wreak havoc and hardship; for instance, if Social Security Administration employees went on strike, the monthly benefits on which many of the 36 million beneficiaries depend for their livelihood would be halted. The concern is clearly legitimate, and yet the recognition that many private employees perform equally important functions weakens this claim as a basis for imposing a strike ban exclusively on federal employees. The federal law could adopt the position already taken by nine state governments and the Virgin Island territories, barring strikes by essential public employees (however defined) while extending to the remainder those rights already enjoyed by workers in the private sector.

It has also been claimed that a prohibition against strikes by federal workers is essential in light of the separation of budgetary and administrative responsibilities in the public sector. In this view, federal management negotiators would find it impossible to respond to a strike threat because the Congress would have to appropriate the additional outlays required under agency bargaining agreements. The separation of budgetary from managerial authority—policy making from policy implementation—occurs in the private sector, although not to the same degree as in government. Still, as a justification for denying federal workers the right to strike, this argument ignores the efforts by state and local administrators to anticipate budget constraints, bargain with unions amid strike threats, and secure any budget adjustments necessary to implement settlements. Of course, the legislatures holding the purse strings may always reject a settlement. But such contingencies may be incorporated as part of the negotiations process, authorizing only conditional settlements by executive managers subject to ratification by Congress.

The sovereignty argument is also invoked in defense of a ban on strikes by federal workers. From this perspective, the strike is an attack on the agency of the people's will, and hence illegal. To some degree the credibility of this stand is mitigated by the fact that union negotiations with the government are authorized by law. If the sovereign is willing to engage in bargaining, by implication the consequences of negotiations should also be recognized. Also, many have found this theory to be not in keeping with a democratic, pluralistic society. If the argument is carried to its logical conclusion, any interest group would be forbidden to pressure the government in pursuit of its objectives, be they altruistic or selfish.

Finally, a prohibition against federal strikes has been supported as an essential protection of democratic processes.[21] The power to strike, according to this view, would place unions in the position of being able to force the sharing of public authority, even though they are private organizations not accountable to the voters. Acknowledging that union actions may in some measure conflict with other democratic processes, others have argued that a trade off is involved. They assert that by encouraging participation on the part of many, who would otherwise remain on the sidelines, unions are advancing democratic processes rather than stifling them.[22]

When viewed collectively, the decision to deny federal workers the right to strike seems less a justifiable response to the unique aspects of federal employee relations than an exercise of unilateral power by politicians. While Congress and the chief executive have been willing to accept collective bargaining as a means of resolving disputes over the bothersome details of labor-management relations, they have never been willing to make themselves vulnerable to the political pressures that would stem from work stoppages in the federal sector. As perceived by federal policymakers, issues of federal pay, hiring, and firing are already sufficiently troublesome in political arenas, and they have little desire to risk the elevation of other employment concerns by granting federal workers the right to strike. Congress has promoted a double standard, insisting that managers in the private sector cope with the threat of work stoppages while remaining unwilling to accept the same constraint on federal officials.

The refusal by political leaders to expose themselves to potential increases in labor-management conflict or political liabilities accounts for the close link between management rights and efficiency in the federal sector. In the private sector, the federal government adopts the role of a relatively neutral referee, and legislates the ground rules for resolving labor-management conflicts with an eye toward achieving a balance between management and worker rights. In the federal sector, the government is both referee and manager. While it attempts to establish impartial arrangements for resolving marginal labor-management issues, it has not been able to resist the temptation of tilting the rules heavily in its own favor. Thus, management rights become indispensable to efficiency in government, and workers are barred from exercising significant clout or addressing the major issues that would render the federal collective bargaining system meaningful.

The self-interested actions of the political managers do not negate the progress made in resolving some worker concerns and grievances through negotiation and arbitration. The creation of netural third parties to arbitrate conflicts in the federal sector has added an important measure of fairness and rationality to federal employee relations during the past decade. However, until the law acknowledges the rights of federal workers, as already enjoyed by their private sector counterparts, federal unions will continue to rely heavily upon lobbying and other political activities to promote worker interests. To do otherwise would be to ignore the political forces that have played a pivotal role in shaping the very structure of federal labor-management relations and that have perpetuated the severe limitations on the representation efforts of organized labor.

4

The Role of the Peace Keepers

Neutral administrative agencies have long been an integral part of private sector as well as state and local labor relations structures. Most lawmakers have recognized the necessity of impartial machinery to settle disputes which would otherwise inundate the courts and overtax their limited expertise in industrial relations. These considerations led Congress to establish the National Labor Relations Board (NLRB) to interpret and administer the 1935 law which required private employers to bargain with worker representatives. The board administers representation elections, determines the appropriate unit for representation (i.e., which employees are eligible to be represented by a particular local or union), and resolves unfair labor practice charges filed by either side. In essence, the NLRB resolves labor-management conflicts and attempts to keep the peace in the private sector.

Given the value of such neutral third parties, it is surprising that these mechanisms have been so late in appearing on the federal scene. The 1962 executive order made no provision for an independent adjudicatory agency; most final decisions on matters involving disputes with unions were left to agency heads, though some cases were resolved by non-binding arbitration. The 1969 order made a halting stab at correcting the situation but still left management in the driver's seat. It established a three-member Federal Labor Relations Council (FLRC) as an appellate policymaking body, but, as indicated earlier, its members were all top presidential advisers and the assistant secretary for labor-management relations was placed in charge of the day-to-day administration of the program. He was given a major role in making bargaining unit determinations and deciding unfair labor practice issues subject to FLRC approval. Responsibility for resolving employee appeals under the merit system remained with the Civil Service Commission.

The 1969 executive order took other incremental steps toward a more balanced and structured labor relations system. Under the order, President Nixon established the Federal Services Impasses Panel (FSIP), an independent body created to handle cases in which labor-management negotiations broke down. Provisions for advisory arbitration of grievances concerning the interpretation or violation of a negotiated contract in the 1962 order were also strengthened to authorize binding arbitration in 1969. Federal employees continued to have access to the statutory appeals system via the Civil Service Commission.

Only with the enactment of the Civil Service Reform Act in 1978 was the interpretation and administration of labor relations statutes placed with a neutral body rather than with management. The three-member FLRC was replaced by the Federal Labor Relations Authority, whose jurisdiction and structure generally resembles that of the NLRB (Figure 3). The authority determines the appropriate unit for purposes of union representation, supervises union elections, and rules on unfair labor practice complaints after they have been adjudicated by an administrative law judge. Perhaps more importantly, the authority also resolves disputes over negotiability and may in limited instances review decisions of arbitrators. The creation of the FLRA lends greater credibility to the overall labor relations program in the federal government.

The 1978 law left essentially unchanged the role of the impasses panel as established by E.O. 11491. The statute grants broad powers to the panel to accept or refuse jurisdiction over disputes, recommend procedures for resolution of impasses, assist the parties, and "take whatever action is necessary . . . to resolve the impasse." The FSIP retains the final say in any contract dispute, and can return cases to the parties for further negotiation, impose a settlement, or turn the case over to an independent arbitrator. The decisions of the FSIP are binding upon the parties unless they reach a separate agreement, and it is an unfair labor practice under the law to refuse to cooperate with the panel.

Notwithstanding the ongoing restrictions on the scope of bargaining in the federal sector, the creation of the FLRA and the FSIP was es-

45

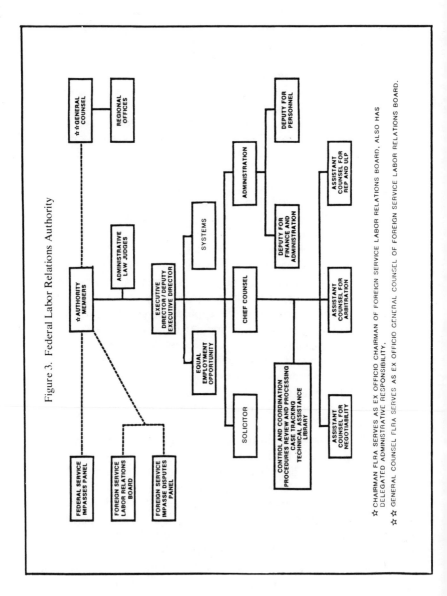

Figure 3. Federal Labor Relations Authority

☆ CHAIRMAN FLRA SERVES AS EX OFFICIO CHAIRMAN OF FOREIGN SERVICE LABOR RELATIONS BOARD, ALSO HAS DELEGATED ADMINISTRATIVE RESPONSIBILITY.

☆☆ GENERAL COUNSEL FLRA SERVES AS EX OFFICIO GENERAL COUNSEL OF FOREIGN SERVICE LABOR RELATIONS BOARD.

sential to the development of independent administrative arrangements, similar to those in the private sector. Rather than being subject to unilateral management rulings, federal unions can present conflicts over the scope of representation and negotiability to an independent third party for a balanced assessment of issues and interpretation of the law. Furthermore, labor has recourse to the impasses panel in the event of deadlocked negotiations, and individual workers can, through their unions, resort to binding arbitration of grievances when they believe their contractual rights have been violated. The role of the peace keepers has ensured a measure of fairness and impartiality in federal labor-management relations. Their presence offers federal workers some protection under the emerging collective bargaining system, and provides an alternative to exclusive dependence on lobbying.

The first and perhaps most important of the issues faced by the parties in a bargaining relationship is the size and scope of the unit involved. In the federal sector, representation questions have dealt primarily with the size and occupational makeup of employee units, the level of management engaged in negotiations with unions, and how far into the management hierarchy a union may reach for members. Resolution of these issues determines the ground rules for subsequent negotiations between management and labor, and thus precedes the addressing of any other bargaining concerns.

Determining the Bargaining Unit

The initial decision in a collective bargaining system is the determination of the appropriate bargaining unit. In the private sector, the NLRB makes such determinations. Initially controversy centered on craft versus industrial unit representation, which was a major factor in the contest between the American Federation of Labor and the Congress of Industrial Unions. More recent adaptations have resulted in geographically based multi-employer units and employer-wide units. The board still tends to prefer units organized within a single plant or facility, but it has adapted its definition of units as the parties have matured.

A parallel development has taken place in the federal sector, but at a less pronounced pace because of the lack of clear preferences on the part of both unions and management. The determination of appropriate bargaining units has traditionally been based on criteria set forth in law, executive orders, or agency regulations. During the emergence of federal unions in the early 1960s, most unions were relatively small and represented only a minority of workers, organized for the most part around craft or occupational groupings. Over the course of the last two decades, however, the trend has been toward increasing consolidation across occupational and geographic lines into agency-wide or even worldwide appropriate units.

Ironically, management and labor preferences regarding the size of appropriate units have almost reversed during the past twenty years, although neither side has adopted a rigid position on the matter. In their formative period, unions sought to define the appropriate unit as narrowly as possible, for they found it easier to organize workers in small and geographically concentrated units. Management, on the other hand, tended to oppose the administrative inconvenience of scattered, small units, and pushed for larger units. Yet, by 1978, the largest federal unions were aggressively pursuing consolidation strategies and advocating larger appropriate units in an effort to strengthen their bargaining power. The unions gain a substantial advantage by first negotiating a national agreement and then bargaining at the local level on more parochial issues. For this reason, many agencies have come to prefer dealing with several small field units rather than with a single, centralized bargaining unit. The strategic calculations of both sides clearly shifted as unions grew in both size and sophistication.

The Kennedy executive order included only vague criteria to guide unit determinations and left final authority for such decisions in the hands of agency heads, with arbitrators in some cases offering advisory judgments. During the first year under the 1962 order, management pushed for larger, more inclusive units in thirty-one of thirty-four cases, taking no position on unit size in the remaining three determinations. In twenty of those thirty-four cases, arbitrators rendered decisions, almost all of which favored smaller units.[1] While agency heads tended to defer to the arbitrator's advice, this difference of opinion reflected an underlying conflict between management and labor perspectives: agency arguments were based on a broad and vague "mission of the facility" criterion for the unit, whereas unions focused on an ill-defined "community of interest" among employees which they felt called for small units.

The clash of views between unions and management continued after the Nixon order established the Federal Labor Relations Council (FLRC) as the ultimate authority on unit determination. The council held that federal policy "should facilitate the consolidation of existing bargaining units."[2] This stance, supported by Executive Order 11616, was demonstrated in a long line of decisions consistently preferring larger to smaller units, and was capped by the FLRC decision in the so-called DCASR Trilogy involving the Defense Contract Administrative Services Region and the American Federation of Government Employees (AFGE). In these three cases, the council overruled unit determinations made by the assistant secretary for labor-management relations, deciding that he had not taken into account important management considerations favoring large units. AFGE was understandably displeased with the council decisions, declaring that "we are favorably disposed to the creation of agency wide or world wide appropriate units, provided that the options for petitioning for smaller appropriate units are not excluded or prohibited."[3]

The Federal Labor Relations Authority, facing different management attitudes and aggressive union consolidation strategies, has replaced the council's approach with a more flexible approach to the size of appropriate units. In a highly complex representation case involving federal employees on the Panama Canal, the FLRA undertook the task of untangling eight separate unions with overlapping memberships and varying bases of representation. In delineating clearer boundaries for appropriate units, the authority approved a unit of all employees of the Panama Canal Commission because of their common mission and function, while disallowing a unit of all nurses because their geographic dispersion resulted in a lack of community of interest. These decisions allowing a kind of "industrial unit" of employees with various skills, however, were offset by the willingness to set up separate units for firefighters and for police officers. In these instances, the authority felt that craft distinctions implied a combination of duties, work schedules, and employee identity sufficiently unique to warrant the establishment of units that crossed agency and geographic lines.[4] More cases will be needed, however, to infer whether the decision was intended to have wider implications.

The authority has attempted to be evenhanded and (within the statutory framework) logically consistent, responding to the specific characteristics of each occupation and work environment by allowing large units in some cases[5] and smaller ones in others.[6] Other FLRA rulings have permitted units spanning several occupations or pay classifications in cases where all employees were engaged in completing the mission of the facility, interaction among them was essential, and they operated under similar personnel rules.[7] At the other extreme, craft has remained a significant criterion in several unit determinations; for example, the authority consolidated all radio broadcasters in one agency into a single NFFE unit rather than placing a few New York City broadcasters within a general AFGE unit based on geographic location.[8]

Labor and management reactions to FLRA determinations of appropriate units have been mixed, reflecting the ambiguity of their evolving preferences and intramural union conflicts. A consistent trend toward broader units would threaten smaller unions that have organized on a narrow craft basis or that are confined to a single facility. Management's position is similarly divided; some agencies prefer agency-wide negotiations and others still favor smaller units. While these internal divisions prevent any overriding push by either management or labor in a single direction, it does appear from recent rulings that the future of the federal labor-management structure lies in larger, consolidated units.

Who Is Management?

In making appropriate unit determinations, the Federal Labor Relations Authority shapes the type of representation that a federal worker receives. In some cases, the FLRA is also required to make judgments on whether a federal employee is entitled to any union representation at all by drawing dividing lines between labor and management. In the federal establishment, decisions as to who is part of management can be even more difficult than in private business, for upper-level managers are often subject to the same civil service statutes and congressional mandates as their subordinates and thereby share many common concerns. The appropriate categorization of supervisors and other middle-level officials is particularly troublesome, and federal labor relations policy as a result has been consistently unclear on whom unions may represent.

The problem stems at least in part from the fact that supervisory duties in the government are harder to define than in the private sector. The blurred line between line and staff personnel, the ever-changing allocation of resources to meet shifting priorities, the lack of coherent work force planning, and the fragmentation of authority all contribute to uncertainty in this area.

Management policy has generally been to exclude as many people as possible from bargaining units. As the Committee for Economic Development argued in a recent statement, supervisors should be considered part of management and "including supervisors in bargaining units with their subordinates, not only confuses the relationship between supervisors and subordinates, but also risks paralyzing government's ability to deal with labor disputes, slowdowns and strikes."[9] In contrast, unions generally seek to organize as far as possible into the management hierarchy, recognizing that such forays tend to isolate upper-level management and strengthen labor's hand at the bargaining table.

Middle-level personnel who are barred from union representation are able to organize around common interests through the formation of professional associations, of which the Federal Management Association and the Professional Management Association are the most prominent. Similarly, the Senior Executive Association represents the interests of the executive service (employees in the upper 3 of the 18 grades with annual pay in 1982 of $57,000 or higher). All these organizations resort to lobbying efforts in Congress and the White House. At times, the distinction between union and professional association grows rather thin, marked primarily by the union's access to formal bargaining rights denied to professional associations. Nevertheless, unions continue to seek inroads into middle-level ranks as a means of bolstering their leverage in areas of direct labor-management confrontation.

The Nixon executive order attempted to provide guidelines for the division between labor and management by enumerating several functions performed on behalf of management that placed federal employees in a supervisory capacity and excluded them from eligibility for union membership. The Federal Labor Relations Council adopted a strict, literal interpretation of the order. Refusing to consider difficult questions involving the degree of supervision, the council concluded that the executive order had "the effect of excluding from the unit any individual who possesses the authority to perform even one of the functions described. . . . This specific standard eliminates degree questions."[10]

The Civil Service Reform Act of 1978 did not significantly alter the order's language regarding supervisors (except in providing for separate treatment of nurses and firefighters), but the Federal Labor Relations Authority has demonstrated a willingness to consider the degree of authority exercised as well as the extent of supervision before determining supervisory status. The FLRA has found, for instance, that some individuals may be supervisors while others with an identical position classification might not qualify, explaining the distinction in terms of location in the agency and the amount of independent authority allowed by the supervisors.[11] The authority has refused to follow the all-inclusive standard adopted by its predecessor in defining supervisory status and chose to deal with the issue on a case-by-case basis. A long line of precedent regarding employees called "small shop chiefs" has also been broken by the authority. The FLRA ruled that these employees were *not* supervisors and that the exercise of authority involves "the consistent use of independent judgment."[12] The number of times an action was taken has been deemed similarly important by the authority.[13]

The FLRA persists with the case-by-case approach of defining management personnel and the unions continue to organize employees with marginal supervisory status. Bargaining may prove more difficult for unions encompassing a greater variety of viewpoints on any given issue. So far the federal unions seem willing to accept this greater diversity in hopes of expanding their overall influence. Presumably unions anticipate that once the supervisors are included in bargaining units, they will act like other union members.

Refereeing the Negotiation Process

Without giving up on lobbying activities, unions have made modest advances through collective bargaining since the passage of the 1978 reform act. When the parties negotiate agreements, the Federal Labor Relations Authority serves as a referee in resolving questions relating to the scope of bargaining. The authority, in its role as peace keeper, is responsible for establishing ground rules of the bargaining process and for ensuring that they are observed by both labor and management.

Paying While on Union Business

A 1971 amendment to the Nixon executive order limited the paid time that union representatives could take for collective bargaining to forty hours or one-half the time spent on negotiations, which placed a limit of twenty hours per week per union representative during each bargaining round. The 1978 reform law removed these limits, however, and required that union representatives be paid for negotiation time and time spent at impasse proceedings. Whether time spent in preparation for these functions is "official" time is open to negotiation. In a rare departure from the authority's usual case-by-case decision making, the

FLRA subsequently issued a policy statement interpreting this language to include travel and per diem expenses for union negotiators.[14]

Unions argue that pay while on union business puts them more nearly on a par with the full-time management representatives. As long as the law proscribes the agency shop, a small percentage of the employees unions represent are dues payers. The unions maintain that if payment for bargaining time were abolished, recalcitrant managers could drag out negotiations and drive unions into bankruptcy.

Management has vehemently opposed a broad grant of paid time for bargaining, complaining that the time needed to reach an agreement has increased dramatically now that unions are no longer dependent upon their own treasuries to support their representatives. For example, bargaining negotiations at the General Services Administration were deadlocked for nearly a year; and at the Social Security Administration and the Veterans Administration it took even longer to reach agreement. As expressed by Anthony Ingrassia, head of labor-management relations in the Office of Personnel Management (OPM), management's concern is that "this shifting of the burden of financial support . . . to the taxpayer could contribute to a potential, if not actual, lack of internal union discipline, responsibility, and a realistic awareness of the labor-management relationship."[15] The FLRA has denied automatic official time to local union officials to negotiate supplemental agreements, making this a matter to be negotiated by the parties to the national agreement.[16] This has not pacified management, however, and the debate continues.

A 1981 OPM rule requires each agency to compile statistics on the cost of official time, but a government-wide reporting of these costs has not yet been made. Preliminary data are available for only two agencies:

Agency	Dates of negotiation	Total cost
Equal Employment Opportunity Commission	September 5, 1979- May 30, 1980	$ 445,140
Social Security Administration	June 10, 1980- December 21, 1981	1,098,787

These estimates cover the *total* cost of negotiations, and fail to report separately costs for union official time, travel, and per diem. Instead, salaries of all management officials and clerical help involved in negotiations have been included in bargaining costs, implicitly assuming that, in the absence of negotiations, these costs would not have been incurred.

53

Useful estimates of official time costs will not be available until OPM breaks down bargaining costs by its major components and collects the data for all federal agencies.

Alternatives to an open-ended official time policy could address labor's legitimate concerns. Allowing unions to collect agency shop fees would be a desirable alternative to the present practice, but would require a change in the law and certainly would encounter stiff opposition in Congress. Another approach would be to limit the time devoted to contract negotiations, leaving the Federal Service Impasses Panel to step in automatically at the expiration of the prescribed bargaining period. This approach is likely to limit the cost for union official time, but it may also discourage agencies and unions from settling disputes on their own, as it may induce either party to rely upon a neutral to settle the dispute. Still, either way, the expiration of the contract would generate some pressure on both sides to resolve differences. Until remedial steps of this nature are taken, past practice suggests that the length of negotiations will continue to grow amid charges by both labor and management that the other side is to blame.

Unfair Labor Practices

A second controversy surrounding the FLRA's role as referee of the negotiations process involves the handling of unfair labor practices (ULP) charges. The substance of the authority's rulings has seldom been at issue. FLRA procedures for handling ULP charges, however, have drawn sharp criticisms from management. The focus of controversy is a provision in the reform act that authorizes the general counsel in the authority's regional offices to process ULP cases and to represent the charging party free of cost in all proceedings.

Pointing to the fact that federal unions now initiate roughly 95 percent of all such cases compared to about 50 percent in the private sector, management charges that free representation by the general counsel removes all constraints from the filing of frivolous ULP charges. According to this view, free representation has opened the entire structure to abuse, encouraging unions to badger management with ULP charges and contributing to a large backlog of cases before the Federal Labor Relations Authority.

Not surprisingly, the unions take a different view of free representation by the FLRA's general counsel staff. They note that their meager treasuries would allow unions to file only a few cases if the general counsel did not act for them, forcing them to pursue only selective justice. Union officials also stress that the ratio of meritorious unfair labor practices as reported by the FLRA is similar to that found by the NLRB in the private sector.[17] Labor considers open access to filing unfair labor practice charges indispensable to a fair collective bargaining structure and a means of ensuring that management respects the unions' limited bargaining rights.

One approach offered to address management's concerns would be to assess a nominal filing fee for each unfair labor practice charge, providing an incentive for settlement without FLRA intervention and stemming the alleged flow of cases filed for nuisance value. The fee should not be imposed as a fine on unions filing more than a certain number of charges, for a system of that nature would penalize larger unions or more vigorous representation while giving agencies with the most transgressions an advantage over their unions.

In the absence of adjustments in ULP procedures, the authority continues to struggle with a heavy, though declining, volume of cases. The general counsel investigates all unfair labor practice charges, and has found an average of 40 percent to be of sufficient merit to warrant issuing a complaint. In some cases, the FLRA has been confronted with tough choices regarding the scope of appropriate remedies when unfair labor practices were documented, particularly when management has already taken an action but refuses to negotiate either its impact or the procedures to be followed during its implementation. For example, in a case involving performance evaluations, the authority rescinded evaluations already completed until the parties had a chance to negotiate over the impact of new evaluation procedures adopted by management.[18] Similarly, in a case involving the reassignment of employees *within* an installation the authority ordered that the employees be returned to their prior status.[19] Yet if the case had involved the moving of agency operators from one city to another (a hypothetical example), status quo remedies would be much more difficult to institute. As the FLRA continues to referee the negotiation process, the problem of reversing or correcting unfair labor practices will continue to plague its enforcement of bargaining rights.

When Negotiations Break Down

The Federal Labor Relations Authority is kept amply busy by merely setting and enforcing the framework for negotiation in the federal sector. The satisfactory resolution of cases involving representation, unfair labor practices, and negotiability is no guarantee of achieving results at the bargaining table. On the contrary, an entirely different role for a neutral peace keeper emerges when labor and management observe collective bargaining procedures but fail to reach agreement. In the private sector, such bargaining impasses usually lead to either binding arbitration or strikes, but in the federal government they have become the purview of the Federal Service Impasses Panel (FSIP).

The creation of the panel in 1969 reflected some unique characteristics of the federal establishment; neither arbitration of contract terms nor strikes were deemed acceptable options. The use of arbitrators from outside the federal establishment in settling contract disputes has long been viewed with a jaundiced eye by lawmakers. There is understandable hesitation in allowing arbitrators to decide issues binding the government when they need not be responsible to the public or its representatives.

The involvement of a neutral party in bargaining impasses was a significant concession to unions, whose officials were adamant that agency heads not have the final say when negotiations broke down. Since they are forbidden to strike, unions sought assurances that differences would not always be settled in management's favor. While unions have been far from convinced that the impasses panel provides an adequate substitute for the right to strike, some have justified its existence as a quid pro quo for the many constraints which the law imposes on organized federal labor. The panel, consisting of members presumably expert in collective bargaining issues, is authorized to employ a wide range of approaches in seeking to resolve bargaining impasses. It can simply issue recommendations for settlement, refer the dispute to outside binding arbitration, or impose specific contract language on the parties. The panel has proven generally reluctant to entrust substantive decisions to an arbitrator outside the government, going along with binding arbitration to resolve impasses only in 10 out of 168 cases disposed during fiscal year 1981 (Table 2). Concerns about the absolute right of government to manage as well as the accountability for government funds when awards involve expenditures may also be causes to

Table 2. Disposition of FSIP cases has changed radically

	1970-77	1978	1979*	1980	1981
Cases received	333	107	96	123	191
Disposition					
Total	287	128	76	132	168
Withdrawn	117	54	33	33	38
Jurisdiction declined	64	21	18	35	37
Settled prior to panel report and recommendation	67	22	11	16	5
Settled after panel report and recommendation	31	9	3	4	5
Decision and order issued	8	19	10	35	73
Arbitration recommended or directed	0	0	0	3	6
Use of arbitration approved	0	2	0	2	4
Use of arbitration not approved	0	1	1	4	0

Source: "Second Annual Report of the Federal Labor Relations Authority and the Federal Services Impasses Panel" (Washington: Government Printing Office, 1980), p. 73; and FSIP office for fiscal 1981.
*January 1 to September 30, 1979.

keep contract impasses in-house.[20] In contrast, since the adoption of the 1978 reform legislation the number of instances in which the panel used its full powers to impose specific contract language on the parties has risen sharply, from an average of one a year between 1970 and 1977 to 73 cases, or 43 percent of all cases closed, in fiscal 1981.

Numerous explanations have been offered for the sharp rise in imposed settlements in recent years. Some note that, because most of the "easy" issues have been resolved in prior cases, the FSIP increasingly faces complex questions on which labor and management are sharply divided, leaving little room for mediation and compromise. With the parties more experienced in the art of collective bargaining, the panel is more likely to be forced to dictate the terms of contract agreements on intransigent negotiators.

Others point to the rising caseload and dwindling staff resources as the causes of more frequently imposed settlements. As a result of Carter and Reagan budget cuts, the panel's full-time staff of nine has been cut to five employees. More important, lacking travel funds for on-site fact-finding and personal contacts, which provide opportunities for mediation, the panel has been forced to rely heavily on written arguments and briefs. Even though the Federal Mediation and Conciliation Service may still intervene in disputes before they reach the panel, it seems clear that the push for a reduced government presence has given the FSIP no alternative but to impose more settlements.

Panel members and staff have made a conscious effort to utilize the full range of options available to them in an attempt to prevent labor and management from turning to the panel every time they encounter a bargaining snag. In describing the concern of this "narcotic effect," the executive director of the panel has testified: "The Panel will try to remain as unpredictable as possible. This flexibility, we certainly hope, will put greater pressure on the parties to bargain harder and thus avoid coming to us. And in this manner [the narcotic effect], which agencies similar to the Panel sometimes have on collective bargaining should remain absent in the Federal labor relations system."[21] Thus far, however, if the panel's caseload is any indication, the parties have displayed a growing reliance on the FSIP. The number of cases brought to the panel has grown steadily since 1979 and currently shows no signs of reversal. In 1981 about one of every ten cases involving potential disputes was brought to FSIP.

The broader effectiveness of the Federal Services Impasses Panel has also been questioned, most frequently by union representatives. Much of the dissatisfaction with the panel's role stems from the fact that it is often unable to address the real issues or hidden agenda underlying bargaining impasses, issues that may not be negotiable under federal collective bargaining statutes. As Howard Gamser, the former chairman of the FSIP, pointed out about the air traffic controllers' 1981 dispute, "Neither [side] indicated any interest in using the Panel's services. They expressed a concern, shared by me and my colleagues on the Panel, that we would be unable to address the merit of the key economic issues in the dispute . . . because they were so clearly beyond the scope of bargaining permitted by the statute."[22] If the issue presented to the panel is not the one that actually has triggered the impasse, there is little hope that the panel can play an effective role; the problem lies with the more basic statutory restrictions on the negotiation process itself.

The establishment of the FSIP, with its power to make final determinations and impose settlements when negotiations falter, was itself an important recognition that the concept of sovereignty in federal labor-management relations has outlived its usefulness. Since the step toward arbitration by a neutral third party has been taken, more comprehensive provisions for the use of arbitrators or arbitration panels operating with reasonable guidance from the Congress now seem warranted. The alternative course will leave the Federal Services Impasses Panel increasingly burdened with cases to analyze and resolve for which it has too few resources and too many constraints.

Abiding by the Contract

The role of the peace keepers does not end with the acceptance of a negotiated agreement. The parties to collective bargaining cannot foresee changing circumstances or anticipate disputes regarding its interpretation. Hence the administration of negotiated contracts is an important element in the quality of union-management relationships. The significance of contract administration has been heightened by the fact that many of the major battles of labor relations that were once fought across the bargaining table have now moved to the grievance/arbitration process. Contract administration, in the words of one leading analyst, "becomes the arena for determining how these provisions actually are applied and what costs and benefits result from the written language."[23]

The method generally used in the private sector to resolve such disagreements is that of submitting the question to an impartial person or panel, and agreeing to abide by whatever decision is reached. This practice of relying upon neutrals has taken on added importance in the private sector because of National Labor Relations Board decisions which have made clear that the resolution of grievances referred to arbitrators may not be later appealed to the NLRB. Thus arbitration in the private sector is a more or less independent system, providing a widely used means of resolving conflicts over the interpretation or violation of a contract. The fact that the courts will rarely overturn an arbitration award has further encouraged reliance upon arbitrators to settle grievances arising out of collective bargaining agreements.

In the federal sector, broad worker rights of redress through grievance arbitration were granted only belatedly. The Nixon executive order allowed negotiated agreements to include provisions for grievance procedures, but processes established by contract could not cover matters for which statutory remedies existed. The order permitted binding arbitration, but "advisory" awards, subject to veto by the agency or department heads, were called for in some contracts. Both were subject to

Federal Labor Relations Council review. The Civil Service Reform Act finally established the right of federal employees to seek relief through either statutory appeal or negotiated grievance procedures (but not both), and mandated that such negotiated procedures include arbitration as a final step should settlement efforts fail. In addition, Section 7103 of the law, while continuing to exclude arbitration of such issues as pay and fringe benefits, broadened the definition of "grievance" to include "any complaint . . . by any employee, labor organization, or agency concerning: (1) the effect or interpretation, or a claim of breach, of a collective bargaining agreement; or (2) any claimed violation, misinterpretation, or misapplication of any law, rule, or regulation affecting conditions of employment."

These revisions of civil service statutes represented important gains for federal workers, although they did not place arbitration rights in the federal sector on a par with those in the private sector. The broad language of the CSRA continues to be limited sharply by other laws dealing with prohibited political activities (Hatch Act restrictions), pay or benefits, firing, hiring, and classification of positions that does not result in reduction in pay or grade. The federal unions also fell short of their goal of binding arbitration subject only to court review (similar to that in the private sector and several state governments), since arbitration awards in the federal sector may still be altered or overturned by the Federal Labor Relations Authority, although the latter's action can be appealed to the courts. As in other areas, the reform legislation provided an expanded role for impartial third parties in the arbitration process, while continuing to view the federal establishment as unique and requiring modifications of the private sector labor-relations model.

The role of arbitration was also enhanced in 1978 by the adoption of statutory limitations on the grounds for appeal of an arbitrator's award. Although the FLRA, the Merit Systems Protection Board (MSPB), the Equal Employment Opportunity Commission (EEOC), and the courts each have jurisdiction in some cases, the grounds for appeal to each of these bodies are limited both by the Civil Service Reform Act (Section 7123) and their own rules and precedents. The courts, for example, may be resorted to only after the ruling of the authority in cases involving an unfair labor practice or discrimination, and even then they are bound in most circumstances by the findings of fact made by the FLRA.

The 1978 statute (Section 7122) allows either party to appeal an arbitrator's decision, and permits the Federal Labor Relations Authority to sustain a petition to overturn or modify an award on the basis of its conflict with laws, rules, regulations, or on "grounds similar to those applied by Federal courts in private sector labor-management relations." Through its rulings, however, the authority has placed great weight upon an arbitrator's decision and has demonstrated reluctance to consider appeals of such awards. Out of the 105 appeals from arbitration awards the FLRA handled during its first three years, it modified 9 awards and in only one instance returned the award to the arbitrator. Its complete record was:

FLRA action	Fiscal 1979-1981
Number of cases appealed to FLRA on merits	105
Sustained award	83
Set aside	10
Modified	9
Remanded	1

The authority has been unwilling to define or utilize the broad power it has under Section 7122 of the law to "take such action and make such recommendations concerning the award as it considers necessary." It has refused, barring egregious error, to review the arbitrator's findings of fact.[24] Only occasionally has it utilized its powers in fashioning an unusual remedy: for example, in one case it ordered that a wronged employee be promoted at the next available opportunity.[25] Generally, however, the FLRA has sought to ensure the legitimacy of arbitration by sharply limiting the appeals that could undermine its finality.

Finally, the Civil Service Reform Act strengthened the arbitration process by providing for more stringent remedies than were previously available. By amending the Back Pay Act, the statute allowed arbitrators and the FLRA to award back pay and attorney fees following a determination that management acted unjustly. With the ability to loosen the purse strings of agencies, both arbitrators and the FLRA have a greater chance of being able to redress grievances in meaningful ways.

Yet the FLRA has had to apply the rather strict standards required by law which limit the power of arbitrators to award back pay.[26] It has ruled that in order to award a retroactive promotion and/or back pay, the arbitrator must find, first, that there has been an "unwarranted and unjustified personnel action," and second, that "but for" this action the employee would have received the promotion or pay.[27] In other words, there must be a direct causal relationship between the disputed manage-

Table 3. Arbitration Awards, 1946-81

Year	Binding	Advisory	Total
1964	—	1	1
1968	—	31	31
1972	53	57	110
1973	81	18	99
1974	148	24	172
1975	254	18	272
1976	318	10	328
1977	457	4	461
1978	479	3	482
1979	580	4	584
1980	759	1	760
1981	740	0	740

Source: Office of Personnel Management.

ment action and the denial of a promotion or pay. A simple finding of neglect on the part of management to carry out duties imposed upon it by the agreement (such as properly instituting a career ladder plan) is insufficient to warrant retroactive compensation.[28] The authority has not included payment of interest in the determination of back pay awards.

Largely because of the liberalized grievance procedures, the use of arbitration has skyrocketed since the early 1970s (Table 3). Even before the passage of the 1978 legislation, which made arbitrators' decisions final, the parties had rarely utilized advisory procedures. Most binding arbitrations continue to be initiated by federal unions and tend to be heavily concentrated in a few federal agencies; limited data collected by OPM indicate that 85 percent of all awards during the past two decades involved only 12 percent of all bargaining units. From 1962 through 1981, unions won 39 percent of all cases as well as 39 percent of cases they initiated while management won 42 percent of the cases they brought to arbitration, and 55 percent overall.

The scarcity of data on arbitration cases makes it difficult to assess the impact of specific changes in arbitration procedures. The CSRA, which took effect in January 1979, no doubt contributed to the sizable increases in the next two years in the number of cases. The slowdown evident in 1981 is somewhat harder to explain. It might be due to the increasing cost of the procedure (over $1,100 per case in 1981),[29] for unions are normally expected to bear 50 percent of arbitration costs.

Yet it is also possible that the decline in case volume stems simply from shifts in union priorities or from disappointment with prior awards.

The evidence does suggest that, at the bargaining table at least, unions have taken advantage of their new rights to include arbitration clauses into their agreements. Between January 1979 and September 1, 1980, 452 agreements were executed and reported to OPM. Thirty-six percent included all of the statutorily permissible areas of appeal in their grievance-arbitration procedures; only one percent limited grievance procedures to the interpretation of the contract. The rest either included only a few of the permissible subjects or did not deal with the subject at all.[30]

In its first three years, the FLRA has not made clear which rules and regulations may govern or limit an arbitrator's award. It has found that government-wide rules, as in the negotiability area, are controlling. What remains ambiguous is the degree to which an agency's own rules may bar findings of error or remedies. Yet both the statute and the authority have left little doubt as to the broader rights of federal workers to seek a redress of grievances before a neutral third party, and the handling of arbitration cases remains one of the most direct ways in which federal unions protect and serve their members.

Are the Peace Keepers Effective?

In theory, there is a close relationship between the presence of neutral third parties in a collective bargaining system and the relative tranquility of labor-management relations. In practice, threats to the fairness and impartiality of the system are far more prevalent. The element of justice in federal employee relations depends not only upon adequate statutory protections of the rights of all parties, but also upon appropriate measures of integrity, judgment, and resources within those entities which fulfill the role of peace keepers. In this broad sense, it seems important to consider how effective the Federal Labor Relations Authority and the Federal Services Impasses Panel in particular have been in overseeing the operation of the federal collective bargaining system.

On the whole, the FLRA appears to have been successful in maintaining an evenhanded approach to labor-management disputes. Although it may have found itself more often on the side of unions, particularly in the area of representation, any charges that it is uniformly pro-union have been rendered less credible by its decertification of the

Professional Air Traffic Controllers Organization following the union's 1981 strike and other less publicized cases. Unions tend to charge that the FLRA has been reluctant to exercise the full powers granted to it; management complains it has often gone too far. Perhaps, as member Henry Frazier has ruefully suggested, attacks from both sides indicate that the authority is, for now, fulfilling its purpose as a neutral arbiter.

If there is a reasonable complaint regarding the substance of FLRA rulings, it is that the authority has been somewhat tentative in its decisions and excessively concerned with the development of a consensus among its members. There is a widespread perception that the members are being extraordinarily careful and that they are reluctant to move on controversies that may wind up in court. The newness of federal sector arrangements and the limited number of precedents to guide its actions have contributed to the FLRA's cautiousness. Its difficulties are accentuated by the propensity of its members to deliver unanimous decisions, necessarily sacrificing some clarity or substance of the decision in the process. During the first three years the authority issued unanimous decisions with one exception. The only dissent (by Chairman Ronald Haughton) was on a procedural issue, and in the PATCO case there was a temporary dissent (the chairman joined the decision to decertify the union when PATCO refused to call off its strike). Both sides have criticized the FLRA for seeking unanimity on controversial issues.

A second, more pressing concern acknowledged by the authority is the large backlog of cases awaiting settlement in the FLRA. The authority inherited the problem from its predecessor agencies, primarily the assistant secretary of the Labor Department, and the apparent intention of both parties to challenge many statutory precedents has caused the backlog to grow steadily during its first three years of operation. President Reagan's fiscal 1982 and 1983 budget cuts, which have already forced the authority to fire forty-eight people—15 percent of the staff —will seriously exacerbate the problem and may place the FLRA permanently far behind in its caseloads. The time lag stemming from this backlog tends to hurt unions more than management. Delays in holding elections, processing unfair labor charges, and confirming arbitration awards undermine worker morale and frustrate union efforts. Management seldom has as much at stake in the timely consideration of FLRA cases.

In 1982 the average processing time for FLRA cases ranged, depending upon the type of case, from eight to fourteen months. Defenders of the authority have accurately noted that this waiting time, although considerable, is often shorter than that experienced in comparable cases before the National Labor Relations Board. For example, 1980 caseloads were processed as follows:

	NLRB	FLRA
Cases pending (approximate)	20,000	1,000
Median processing period—days on cases that receive hearings		
Unfair labor practices	483	291
Representation	263	237
Negotiability	—	420
Arbitration appeals	—	270

The usefulness of this type of comparison, however, is limited by the FLRA's mandate also to consider negotiability and arbitration appeals, which are outside of the NLRB's jurisdiction, as well as by the unique problems of the federal sector. With federal unions denied so many of the bargaining rights enjoyed by their private sector counterparts, they must rely more heavily on negotiability and arbitration challenges, thus making the FLRA's backlog a greater threat to the unions' cause.

The FLRA has considered steps to reduce the backlog but has delayed instituting new procedures. Under one proposal the authority would delegate final authority for most unfair labor practice cases to the administrative law judges (ALJs) who first decide the cases. The authority has taken halting steps in this direction by dropping its review of ALJ decisions in instances where neither party objects to the outcome. This is generally seen as a preliminary step to routinely accepting ALJ decisions, even over objections, absent compelling evidence of error. Although such cases are handled in a similar way by the NLRB, the federal law is unclear on the extent of responsibility the FLRA may delegate, and therefore a complete "sign off" procedure may be vulnerable to court challenge.

Another proposal to reduce the unfair labor practice caseload is to channel a large proportion of cases into arbitration by placing a hold on unfair labor practice cases while the parties try to settle some grievances through arbitration. (This would apply, of course, only to those cases that are allowed to travel this route by law.) The authority, if it chose, could then defer to the arbitrator's decision and relieve itself of at least part of the burden of unfair labor practice cases, and objections by either side to the arbitration award could still be heard through arbitration appeals. The problem with this suggestion is the cost to unions to pursue the same cases, since unfair labor practice handling is free whereas arbitration is not. More importantly, it is not clear that the federal statute allows such action, since the law explicitly offers employees a choice between authority and arbitration processes on issues susceptible to resolution under either procedure (Section 7116-D). If the FLRA were to block either path, even temporarily, its action would certainly be open to a court challenge.

Negotiability cases also contribute to the logjam experienced by the authority, though the problem is not so severe as it was during the first year of operation. Because negotiability determinations are unique to the federal sector, there is little precedent for the authority or its staff. These cases come to the authority *de novo,* and the legality of interposing intermediate steps between the parties and the FLRA is not clear, since the statute does not appear to provide for them. Some efforts have been made in this direction, but they have been unsuccessful. The FLRA tried, for example, to work with the Federal Mediation and Conciliation Service to set up a group of mediators with experience in the federal sector. This group might then be called in to mediate when the negotiability of a proposal was in dispute. These efforts failed, however, because of internal FMCS structure, and have contributed to FLRA's failure to issue timely negotiability decisions, a major weakness in the dispute resolution process.

The Federal Services Impasses Panel has shared the FLRA's problems of inadequate resources, leading to the rise of imposed settlements noted earlier. Yet the strongest challenge to the FSIP's effectiveness lies not in the timeliness of its actions, but rather in the sharply limited scope of its jurisdiction. In many ways, the panel is outside the mainstream of labor-management conflict, able to address only issues that are negotiable, but most conflicts stem from concerns outside of statutory boundaries for bargaining. There seems little that the FSIP can do to bolster its effectiveness in this regard, but it is incumbent upon the Congress to develop impasse mechanisms that have more potential usefulness in coping with the practical rather than theoretical causes of serious contract disputes. This implies a willingness to reexamine the limits on bargaining which are in part responsible for impasses.

Meanwhile, some observers contend that outside arbitration would be a more effective vehicle for resolving bargaining impasses. While state and local experiences with arbitration have not been conclusive, they do suggest that these procedures can be reconciled with government's exercise of constitutional responsibilities and decision-making authority. Most state legislatures give a great deal of guidance to arbitrators on the issues that they may cover in their awards, and congressional directives governing FSIP actions have already illustrated the applicability of this approach at the federal level. If one assumes that the Congress willingly "delegates" its powers to arbitrators within carefully prescribed guidelines, arbitration awards could be defended as both constitutional and final in all but the most unusual circumstances. Moreover, continued guidance resulting from review by the courts should allay concerns over the excessive delegation of power to arbitrators.

Both the FLRA and FSIP have performed reasonably well in utilizing the resources and opportunities made available to them. With their presence, collective bargaining has taken on added significance in the federal sector, providing orderly procedures for resolving labor-management conflicts that occur within the narrow realm of negotiability. Yet the bulk of important issues in federal employee relations remain off the bargaining table and outside the purview of the neutral peace keepers, largely because these issues are of concern to interest groups who are not part of the collective bargaining system. Only the Congress and the White House, through political processes, can mediate among federal workers, managers, and those outside political lobbies. Thus federal employee relations will probably continue to be a hybrid of limited negotiations and repeated interventions or resolutions through political action.

5

The Attempt to Rationalize Federal Pay

Political leaders have been reluctant to grant federal workers the right to bargain over wages. Nor has there been sustained union pressure to obtain the right. Believing that such an extension of bargaining rights would provide inadequate protection for the public interest, the competing demands of federal employees and the taxpayers repeatedly have been weighed in the political realm and compensation set through the normal budgetary process by executive and legislative actions. This structure permits all interest groups who have a stake in federal pay to influence the determination of wages through political lobbying efforts. Compromises are made and conflicts are generally resolved on the basis of which group has the loudest voice. In recent years, as concern over budget deficits has been paramount, union members and all other employees have been the losers in this process.

Yet there remains an abiding interest in the development of more rational mechanisms for determining federal pay. While establishing compensation through political action functions as a last resort for resolving conflict, this system is inadequate in several respects. From a traditional management perspective, the haphazard political resolution of compensation issues is antithetical to any rational long-range planning, and provides no assurance that the federal government will attract and retain qualified workers. Perhaps more importantly, the current system leaves the Congress and the White House at the center of disputes over federal pay, with minimal resort to standards of equity or necessity that might justify their actions. Thus, for reasons of management efficiency and political expediency, the federal government's "board of directors" has continuing incentives to move the determination of wages from the political arena into a more independently functioning system.

The Congress has responded to these managerial and political concerns by identifying wages in the private sector as the appropriate reference point for federal pay. Rather than attempting to choose any independent notion of a "just rate of pay" for federal workers, it has endorsed the concept of comparability as a vehicle for allowing the private market to make that determination. In a managerial context, the idea is to set federal compensation high enough to attract and retain qualified employees without distorting wage rates in the labor market as a whole. While comparability prevents government pay from seriously lagging behind private sector scales, it implicitly relegates the government to a follower's role—a role that accounts for the concept's broad political appeal. Comparability guarantees that federal workers are being paid only as much as they are worth in the private labor market, and it offers hope of removing compensation issues from political realms through routine calculations of average private sector wages and corresponding adjustments in federal pay scales.

In concept, comparability has won general acceptance in recent years as the appropriate frame of reference in determining federal compensation. For federal unions, comparability has offered a way of linking their members' pay to wage gains secured in the private sector, and it also provides some objective basis for wage hike demands that are unpopular with taxpayers and many members of Congress. For federal managers, comparability serves as a guidepost in agency planning and budgeting as well as offering some leverage in seeking to retain experienced personnel. Finally, for political leaders, comparability gains its appeal from its common-sense relationship to "fair" pay, minimizing political disputes over the appropriate size of pay increases and ideally removing such adjustments from day-to-day political considerations.

The attempt to design pay systems that operate independently and objectively while allowing for input from unions, managers, budget officials, and other authorities has led to the development of several scales in the federal establishment. Most blue collar workers are classified under the Federal Wage System, which provides for the coparticipation of union and management in setting the ground rules for wage surveys in the private sector. Most white collar employees are covered by the General Schedule, under which comparability recommendations are made by a pay agent comprised of presidential advisers. The two major pay systems cover 93 percent of the 2.1 million full-time nonpostal federal employment. Thus, while comparability remains the central standard by which all federal pay is determined, the actual process of establishing pay scales varies according to the individual pay system.

The Federal Wage System

The 450,000 federal blue collar workers, accounting in 1982 for nearly one-fifth of the total federal civilian work force, have their wage rates set largely by the Federal Wage System (FWS). The majority of these blue collar employees are organized and 86 percent are represented by unions. Two of every three blue collar jobs are in the Department of Defense, making it by far the largest employer of blue collar workers; the Veterans Administration, next in size, accounts for only 7.4 percent of the blue collar work force.[1]

Before 1967, the wages of blue collar workers were set by local boards within each agency (hence the term "wage-board employees"). These agency boards collected wage data in a number of specified labor markets, obtained the opinions of employee groups, and, based on these data, set wages for the agency and area in which they operated.[2] Due to significant differences in job descriptions as well as methods of data collection, pay rates for essentially the same job varied widely among federal agencies in each area.

The unions were for the most part satisfied with the decentralized pay system, since they were able to exert a great deal of pressure on many agencies in the determination of wage scales. A unified system would have been, in their view, much less open to their influence. From the 1940s until 1967, federal unions succeeded in preventing any legislative or executive action adopting a more centralized pay policy for blue collar workers.

In 1965 President Johnson directed the Civil Service Commission (CSC) to develop a coordinated federal wage system which would ensure uniform federal pay rates for similar jobs in each geographic area. As in the approach of the wage boards, the new pay system was based on the concept of "prevailing wage." The Civil Service Commission was given centralized responsibility for developing general survey policies with the advice of management and union representatives. The wage surveys were to be carried out by the Bureau of Labor Statistics (BLS), but final approval of pay scales rested with the director of the CSC. This revised structure was implemented in 1967.

A year later, in 1968, Congress intervened. The Monroney amendment to a Post Office appropriations bill required that occupational wage surveys include data from the nearest area in which comparable work was performed. The situation that prompted the amendment was competition for skilled machinists between an air force installation which overhauled planes in Oklahoma City and a private airline in Tulsa with a similar facility. Though the two cities were not in the same wage area for the purposes of a survey, they competed for skilled workers outside their immediate labor markets. Monroney's amendment required Tulsa wage data to be figured into Oklahoma City wage surveys. This revision, albeit justifiable in union eyes, represented the first step away from a strictly defined local prevailing wage principle in the blue collar pay system.

In 1972, under pressure from executive agencies, Congress overhauled the wage system in a way that represented a major victory for federal unions representing blue collar workers. The new system tied in-grade pay increases to longevity rather than merit, enabling blue collar workers to progress within each grade automatically over time in all the fifteen grades. While unions were unsuccessful in securing adoption of the ten in-grade steps enjoyed by federal white collar workers, they did manage to raise the number of steps from three to five.

The new law retained the "area prevailing wage" concept, but the methods by which this principle is put into practice, and the deep involvement of the unions in the process, may have served to bias federal blue collar pay upward. The unions were able to restrict pay surveys to better paying private (as opposed to public sector) employers, and to require payment of shift differentials to federal workers regardless of local private sector practice. While the minimum size of firms is not dictated by statute, the administrative costs of pay surveys have resulted in current rules limiting surveys to firms of at least 50-100 or more employees, depending on the industry, thereby including more large firms whose wages are typically higher than those of smaller companies. In addition, this size limitation tends to bias survey samples toward metropolitan rather than rural firms, further raising the surveys' average

71

wage calculations. All these elements of survey structure have ensured that technical aspects of determining blue collar wage rates will remain a source of considerable controversy.

The unions have also secured a central role in the establishment of survey policies governing how and where the pay surveys will be conducted, and which occupations will be covered by each survey. Both the unions and the appropriate section of OPM formulate recommended survey policies, which are then presented to the prevailing rate advisory committee (PRAC), made up of five union and five management representatives and headed by a chairman appointed by OPM. This committee in turn designs its own survey policy (based on the recommendations of the parties), which is at last submitted to the director of OPM, to be accepted, modified, or rejected.

For each geographic area, OPM designates a "lead agency" (the one employing the most blue collar employees), responsible for developing a survey strategy and promulgating a rate structure which is followed by all other federal agencies in the area.[3] The survey is updated annually in each of the 135 wage areas throughout the United States. The union representing the most blue collar employees in each area is the "lead union," and carries a great deal of weight in policymaking, even though OPM has final say on regulations controlling the process. At all levels of survey policy development and implementation, the unions' right to name voting members to the three key advisory and functional committees ensures that they have a great deal of input.

The Carter and Reagan administrations have attempted since 1979 to amend, if not overhaul, the system by which blue collar wage rates are determined. First, the Reagan administration has favored the repeal of the Monroney amendment, contending that by expanding the survey beyond labor market areas, employers who are not truly a part of the competition for employees are included. Unions in turn insist that the relevant labor market is that which contains the comparable jobs, no matter how far away the competing employer is—an argument that might be more persuasive if more blue collar jobs operated in a national or regional labor market.

Second, the administration seeks to reduce the number of within-grade pay steps to the prevailing two or three steps in the private sector. In 1982 OPM undertook a review of the progression procedures. In the Federal Wage System, the five steps currently range from 96 percent to 112 percent of comparability, with step two being 100 percent of the prevailing wage. Progression to the top step is automatic and achieved within six years. Predictably, the unions bitterly oppose any reduction in the number of steps, pointing to the white collar general schedule with its ten within-grade steps as an appropriate model for blue collar employees. Of course, unions also oppose any restriction on the automatic raises within grades.

Finally, the administration seeks to broaden the scope of the FWS surveys to include state and local public employment in each wage area, arguing that these agencies compete with the federal government for blue collar workers. Since state governments tend to be lower-wage employers than the federal government, the unions generally oppose their inclusion in the surveys.

As of mid-1982, blue collar unions have been able to prevent the administration proposals from reaching the floor of either chamber, an indication that unions have not completely lost their influence in Congress over wage issues. The decentralized structure of the FWS has contributed to the union success in forestalling rule changes, for a single standard of comparability as exists in the white collar system would be more visible and easier to modify than many diverse practices without central coordination. In addition, because federal blue collar workers have lower average wages and comprise a smaller portion of the federal work force than their white collar counterparts, pay raises of blue collar workers tend to be far less costly.

In 1982 a one percent increase in the FWS would have cost approximately $90 million compared to $300 million for a similar rise in white collar pay. With blue collar workers being represented in a substantially greater proportion than white collar employees, and with blue collar unions more closely tied to the AFL-CIO, organized labor has had more clout in battles over blue collar pay than in disputes over wages for white collar employees.

The recent imposition of a blue collar pay cap—limiting increases to that allowed for white collar workers under the general schedule—has stimulated political activity among unions representing blue collar workers. Although the survey process continues to churn out comparisons for the purposes of comparability, the results increasingly are ignored, and each grade receives the pay increase allowed by the annual federal budget. Tying federal blue collar wage adjustments to white collar increases and limiting both to a level below comparability has, inevitably, led to reinvigorated politicization of the pay issue.

The General Schedule

The pay schedule covering the largest bloc of employees in the federal service is the general schedule (GS). About 1.4 million white collar workers are included in the eighteen-grade pay scale, whose origins date back to the Classification Act of 1939. During the succeeding two decades pay increases voted by the Congress resulted in a compression of the federal salary structure relative to that of the rest of the economy, and only in the seven lowest grades did average salary keep pace with rises in cost of living as measured by the Consumer Price Index. As a result, federal pay began to lag seriously behind wage rates in the private sector: in 1962 the average gap ranged from 18 percent for a clerical worker to 38 percent for a top federal manager. A series of legislative actions in the 1960s corrected internal salary relationships, distorted by slow wage growth at upper grade levels, and eliminated the average gap between federal and private sector pay.[4]

Having corrected the wage inequities, Congress tried to place the responsibility for annual pay adjustments on the shoulders of the executive branch by passing the 1970 Federal Pay Comparability Act. The Congress was emphatic in its mandate: "Federal pay rates [must] be comparable with private enterprise pay rates for the same levels of work."[5]

The primary responsibility for the interpretation of the act lies with the pay agent, consisting of the directors of the Office of Management and Budget and the Office of Personnel Management, and the secretary of labor. This body selects the five union members of the Federal Employees' Pay Council to serve in an advisory function. The Bureau of Labor Statistics provides technical expertise and is responsible for carrying out the annual private pay survey, known as the professional, administrative, technical, and clerical (PATC) survey, according to the rules designed by the pay agent. The pay agent recommends a pay adjustment, comparable to findings in the private sector, based on the results of the PATC survey. The president, with the advice of the independent three-member advisory committee on federal pay, may either accept the recommendation—in which case it goes automatically into effect—or design an alternative which is submitted to Congress. If the alternative is rejected by either house, the original comparability adjustment recommended by the pay agent goes into effect (Figure 4).

Figure 4. White collar pay determination

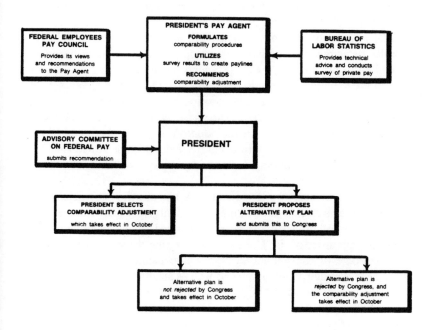

Source: U.S. Department of Labor, Bureau of Labor Statistics, Monthly Labor
Review, June 1979, p. 18.

As in the case of the FWS, the implementation of comparability in
the general schedule is plagued by technical issues which go to the heart
of the pay system. The process by which the pay agent constructs the
"payline" involves a complex set of calculations that weights various
elements of the surveys (such as proportions of workers in each industry
who are employed in large establishments) in order to determine the
average pay for each grade. Present methods appear to be equitable,

especially since the computation of average federal pay in each grade takes into account the distribution of employees within each grade. Apart from their desire to introduce a measure of total compensation comparability, which includes fringe benefits into this calculation, OPM seems satisfied with the current method of fitting the payline to statistical data. Yet even the most skillfully crafted pay scale will be found lacking if it is applied as a single standard for all areas, whether urban or rural with high or low wage levels.

Many of the specific controversies regarding the GS pay scale closely parallel those raised in the FWS. The scope of the surveys, for instance, is limited to private sector establishments, as are those for blue collar pay. This structure in recent years has worked to the advantage of federal employees, because state and local government workers have been slipping in pay relative to private sector workers.[6] While the Reagan administration has argued that the addition of such public sector jobs would make pay surveys more accurate, federal unions have thus far been successful in excluding state and local pay scales from the wage survey.

The scope of current GS pay surveys has also been criticized for geographic bias and an undue emphasis on large private employers. In 1962 surveys of private industry pay included specified industries in metropolitan areas of the United States. During the next two decades the coverage of the annual surveys was expanded to include firms located in nonmetropolitan areas as well as smaller establishments.[7] By 1981 the survey included 43,000 establishments employing 23.6 million white collar workers, focusing on 23 occupations, and covering 96 narrowly defined work levels (Table 4). The surveys still do not reach down to firms with fewer than 100 employees except in accounting firms, and for this reason alone establishments in urban areas tend to be overrepresented, but the PATC surveys clearly have become more comprehensive over the last twenty years.

Unions have objected to any further inclusion of smaller firms on the ground that small firms normally do not have sufficient specialization to permit distinctions in skill levels, and that wage surveys based on occupational classifications in small firms therefore would not reflect skill differences common in the federal government. For example, in a small firm a clerical employee may perform filing, typing, and other office duties, while in a large establishment these functions would more likely fall into distinct, specialized work roles. Nevertheless, critics of the

Table 4. In 1981 the general schedule pay survey included more than 43,000 establishments employing 100 or more persons.

Industry Division	Minimum Employment of Establishment	Number of Establishments
All industries	—	43,238
Manufacturing	100/250 (range)	20,648
Nonmanufacturing:		
Mining	250	635
Construction	250	673
Public utilities	100/250 (range)	4,055
Wholesale trade	100	4,861
Retail trade	250	3,644
Finance, insurance, and real estate	100	6,181
Selected services	50/100 (range)	2,541

Source: Bureau of Labor Statistics, "National Survey of Professional, Administrative, Technical, and Clerical Pay, March 1981" (Washington: Government Printing Office, September 1981), p. 34.

existing survey structure claim that the exclusion of smaller employers renders calculations of average wages both inaccurate and misleading.

At times, the disputes over the technical aspects of implementing the comparability principle call into question the legitimacy of the concept itself. To paraphrase Humpty Dumpty, the meaning of "comparable pay" depends upon what the user of the phrase wants it to mean. While it has been linked to average pay for a given occupation in the private sector, a weighted average which reflects differences in working conditions or fringe benefits might be more appropriate. The definition of "same level of work" is similarly problematic, because selection of private sector jobs where required skills and performance levels match those of federal employees is a complex task under the best of circumstances and is next to impossible when a certain occupation is unique to government. In these instances, the simple notion of comparability masks much more complex issues, and the technical design of pay scales becomes a "back door" method of bargaining over wages by the federal government.

Unions are involved in the GS pay process, but their participation is not so influential as it is for blue collar workers. The views of the federal employees pay council are, according to the 1970 act, to be given "serious consideration" by the pay agent in its annual comparability determination. Yet, this statutory provision has been largely ignored, as

Table 5. Pay comparability, March 1981

	Average Annual Pay	
GS Grade	Private	Federal
1	$ 9,418	$ 8,355
2	10,663	9,486
3	12,043	10,734
4	13,570	12,107
5	15,255	13,611
6	17,107	15,251
7	19,140	17,033
8	21,363	18,960
9	23,787	21,036
10	26,424	23,262
11	29,284	25,639
12	35,710	30,841
13	43,135	36,613
14	51,612	42,897
15	61,172	49,600

Source: President's Pay Agent, "Comparability of the Federal Statutory Pay Systems with Private Enterprise Pay Rates" (Washington: President's Pay Agent, 1981), p. 19.

the council's views seem to have had little effect. Its recommendations on the scope and establishment size to be included in the surveys were accepted during the early 1970s, and in 1977 the pay council helped to get an across-the-board increase rather than a differential pay scheme which would have benefited the top of the pay scale. But when President Carter imposed a pay cap in 1978, the council's members resigned, thus effectively ending any institutional employee involvement. In July 1982 the unions attempted to reactivate the council but without notable success.

Upper level managers have been deprived almost totally of a voice in the determination of salaries. With no representation on the employee council and no institutionalized role in the process, they have suffered the most in recent years (Table 5). By 1981, the comparability increase required for the mass of federal employees receiving less than $25,000 annually was about 12 percent, while those receiving $50,000 and up trailed their civilian counterparts by 23 percent (Figure 5). The gap was particularly serious at the top because of the pay ceiling imposed by Congress. As a consequence of the virtual pay freeze between 1977 and

Figure 5. The higher the grade, the further federal
employees fell behind in comparability

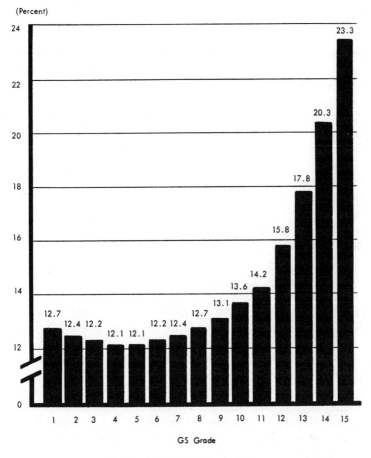

Source: President's Pay Agent, 1981.

1982, senior executives were leaving government service in record
numbers. A 1981 study by the Merit Systems Protection Board found
that 80 percent of executives surveyed felt that the Senior Executive
Service had insufficient incentives to retain qualified employees, and
nearly half stated they were considering leaving the government within

the next two years.[8] Of the 6,500 positions in the SES, there were 930 vacancies created from July 1979 to March 1981.[9]

To the dismay of perhaps all concerned, comparability has proven far more complicated in practice than in concept, and it has yet to spawn an independent and self-adjusting pay-setting structure as originally hoped. The attempt to mirror private sector pay scales has been most successful in blue collar occupations, for which the identification of private sector counterparts is relatively straightforward. The selection of appropriate reference groups for white collar employees in the federal sector, however, has been more troublesome, and even for blue collar workers the treatment of federal fringe benefits has stirred controversies regarding the legitimacy of comparability calculations. Given the ambiguities of the concept and the ever-present political pressure to scapegoat federal workers, comparability may forever be a debating point in the political struggle as part of annual squabbles over the level of the federal budget. Under the best of circumstances, the implementation of the comparability principle required a great deal of pain and care, and both Congress and the executive branches gave up on the system.

The Broken Promise of Comparable Pay

The original intent of Congress in placing the concept of comparability at the core of both blue collar and white collar pay systems was equity. In linking the wages of federal workers to those of similar employees in private industry, the hope was that federal employees could be treated fairly without disrupting or distorting private labor markets. The other clear desire of Congress in passing comparability statutes was to remove itself from the center of perennial disputes over federal compensation which had plagued legislators since the 1800s, and to intervene only in extraordinary circumstances. These political pressures, ones which Congress sought to escape, have prevented the comparability system from operating as the independent system for setting pay envisioned by its sponsors.

In the early 1970s, both blue collar and white collar pay systems functioned without political intervention. Twice, in 1973 and 1974, the White House attempted to use "emergency" procedures, provided in the law, by proposing adjustments to the general schedule lower than those recommended by the pay agent, but the proposals were rejected by the

Table 6. Between 1978 and 1982 annual federal pay recommendations exceeded actual adjustments by 18 percentage points.

Year	Percent CPI Change	Percent Increase in Major Collective Bargaining Agreements	Pay Agent Recommendation	Actual Adjustment
1971	4.3	9.2	6.5	5.5
1972	3.3	6.6	5.1	5.1
1973	6.2	7.0	4.8	4.8
1974	11.0	9.4	5.5	5.5
1975	9.1	8.7	8.7	5.0
1976	5.8	8.1	4.8	4.8
1977	6.5	8.0	7.1	7.1
1978	7.6	8.2	8.4	5.5
1979	11.5	9.1	10.4	7.0
1980	13.5	9.9	13.5	9.1
1981	8.5	9.7	15.1	4.8
1982	6.1	NA	18.5	4.0

Source: Bureau of Labor Statistics, *A Decade of Federal White-Collar Pay Comparability 1970-1980* (Washington: Advisory Committee on Federal Pay, 1981).

Congress. Since that time, political considerations have caused successive presidents and Congresses to subvert the pay process—in 1975, and from 1978 to 1982; alternative pay plans falling well below the pay agent's recommendations have been adopted for GS employees (Table 6). These alternative plans have also affected workers under the Federal Wage System because of the imposition of a pay ceiling linking FWS and GS pay hikes. Notwithstanding their intentions, political leaders have found it difficult to raise the salaries of "bureaucrats" amid rising federal deficits and an unmistakably antigovernment public mood.

Some observers have suggested that "grade inflation" or overclassification has provided indirect pay increases to individuals and groups which offset, in part, the reduction of direct wage boosts. In some cases, grade inflation has been attributed to government position classifiers who recognize underpayment of federal personnel as a real problem. Unions may also fuel upward classification trends in some instances, as in 1976 when the air traffic controllers organization succeeded in using a brief slowdown to secure an increase in grade for air traffic controllers at busy airports. The union claimed that the reclassification was justified by a prior study which the Civil Service Commission refused to implement. Other studies of grade inflation offer alternative explanations wholly unrelated to issues of federal pay, pointing instead to circumstances such as interagency power differences which permit certain agencies to upgrade their personnel.[10] While no single explanation offers solid evidence that classification levels as a whole have climbed in recent years, the concurrent slowdown in direct wage hikes and perceived increase in grade inflation make it difficult to dismiss totally some correlation between these two developments.

Perhaps the more heated debate in the wake of successive alternative pay plans has centered on whether existing pay systems overstate comparability by failing to consider the fringe benefits of employment. Pointing to a favorable contrast in paid holidays, and government guarantee of a subsidized retirement system, management has argued that federal employees are more than adequately compensated. For this reason, the Reagan administration has contended that some measure of total comparability would be a more appropriate reference point for federal pay, in that it would more accurately balance the relative advantages of private and federal employment.

In reviewing the fringe benefits provided to federal workers, there is no question about the generosity of their retirement plan, first established in the 1920s as an independent system supported by employee and employer contributions. The ostensible rule of 50-50 funding (both sides contributing 7 percent of annual wages) masks a true ratio of approximately 35/65 created because the government makes up any shortfall out of general revenue funds.[11] Annuities are based on length of service and the average highest pay during three years, but under no circumstances less than the individual would have received from social security. Benefits are indexed for inflation, although unlike social security payments, federal annuities are taxable. Still as a result of indexing the pay of a federal employee who retired in 1974 doubled by 1982. Employees also do enjoy several retirement options which enable them to qualify for pensions under more generous terms than under social security or most private pensions (Table 7). As a result of the generous pension system the price tag of the federal civilian retirement system reached nearly $18 billion in fiscal 1982.

Comparisons of other fringe benefits suggest that federal employees in general come out ahead. The workers compensation program, for example, has been fairly generous. Since 1974 the benefits paid out under this plan have increased by over 300 percent; in fiscal 1980 alone, $780 million was paid out in disability and medical benefits. Average weekly benefits were $723 in 1981 for federal workers. This was second

Table 7. Retirement Options

Type of Retirement	Minimum Age	Minimum Service (Years)	Special Requirements
Standard	62	5	None
	60	20	None
	55	30	None
	50	20	Law enforcement, firefighter personnel, and air traffic controllers
Optional	Any age	25	Agency must be undergoing a major reduction in force as determined by the Office of Personnel Management
Discontinued service	Any age	25	Separation must be involuntary and not for misconduct or delinquency
	50	20	
Disability	Any age	5	Totally disabled for service in the position occupied

Source: Office of Personnel Management.

only to the benefits in Alaska ($859/week), and vastly more than in all other states, where the average payment was $220/week.

The Office of Personnel Management has attempted to quantify the value of fringe benefits for both federal and private sector workers to permit a broader total comparability. OPM surveyed in 1980 the cost of nonfederal sector benefits and then estimated the cost that would be incurred to provide these same benefits for federal employees, comparing these projected costs with the current cost of federal benefits. The study yielded the following estimates of the value of various benefits in the federal and private sectors:

Benefit	Federal value	Private value
Retirement	28.2% of pay	16.7% of pay
Life insurance	0.3% of pay	0.9% of pay
Secondary benefits	0.3% of pay	5.5% of pay
Health benefits	$903/year	$1242/year
Leave	361 hours/year	351 hours/year

"Secondary benefits" include profit-sharing plans, savings and thrift plans, stock ownership, bonuses, employee discounts, and subsidized cafeterias.

A number of formulas have been devised by OPM and the Congressional Budget Office in attempts to factor these estimates into a measure of total comparability. Depending upon the method used to calculate benefits, the differences in the cost of fringe benefits ranged from

2.8 percent below the cost in the private sector to 7.4 percent in excess of private employees. Yet the overall comparisons remain speculative and controversial. The GAO questioned OPM's estimates that the cost of federal fringe benefits is higher than private outlays for fringe benefits, arguing that "other acceptable approaches would have yielded different results."[12] The uncertain link between the cost of benefits and their value to employees will continue to plague efforts to develop an objective methodology for such comparisons.

Even if the relative value of fringe benefits could be estimated with reasonable accuracy, the Advisory Committee on Federal Pay argued that pay and fringe levels for federal workers should be addressed separately. To deal with pay and benefits as a package, the committee held, would be to perpetuate and institutionalize the lack of balance between salary and benefits—and underpayment of the former—which resulted in the early 1980s in a brain drain from the upper levels of the federal service. The committee stated its belief that "benefits . . . are not interchangeable as motivating factors in improving employee performance and attracting highly qualified employees."[13]

Bills have been introduced in Congress to implement total comparability, but the Reagan administration has added a new twist to the idea. In addition to including fringes in the comparability formula, the proposed legislation would have set federal wages at 94 percent of comparability in order to account for the presumed "intangible benefits" of federal employment. Apparently, the administration believes that the additional security traditionally associated with federal employment, the psychic income of serving one's country, and in some cases the exercise of power all serve to make federal jobs more desirable and could be sufficient to attract competent personnel into the federal establishment despite levels of pay and benefits marginally below those available in the private sector. In support of this claim, the OMB director has stressed in congressional testimony that there were 9.3 applicants for every federal job filled in 1980.

The administration's proposal, later withdrawn, has come under heavy fire from members of Congress, federal unions, and the GAO; each has questioned the administration's assumptions and the arbitrary valuation of intangible benefits at 6 percent of federal pay. Citing 1981 layoffs and disruptions, the General Accounting Office challenged OMB evidence regarding the presumed attractiveness of federal employment.[14] GAO contended that it would be more appropriate to consider the 4 to 1 ratio of applicants to federal vacancies than the higher ratio of applicants to jobs filled used by OMB. The GAO suggested that high unemployment in 1980 probably resulted in similar applicant-to-vacancy ratios in the private sector. Furthermore, GAO noted that the time lag between pay surveys in March and pay adjustments in October already reduced federal pay by roughly 5 percent (based on 1979 and 1980 data), a loss not accounted for in the Reagan proposal for total comparability.

There appears to be a middle ground in comparability determinations, one that would incorporate measurable aspects of relevant fringe benefits while recognizing that wages and benefits are not completely inter- changeable. Those considering employment in the federal sector un- doubtedly weigh the overall pay package, and generous fringe benefits can compensate for somewhat less attractive wages in some cases. If comparability between public and private sector compensation is to remain the dominant pay principle, steps should be taken to make it more logically consistent. Given the Reagan administration's views, it remains to the Congress to take the initative in developing an acceptable comparability formula to achieve this end.

Should Comparability Be the Guide?

By 1982 the debate over the measurement and implementation of comparability has become moot, for it no longer appears to guide federal pay adjustments. In 1982 the raise required to catch up would have been 18.47 percent, and such a one-step implementation of com- plete comparability would have been prohibitively expensive. An 18 percent increase in the total civilian federal wage bill would have amounted to some $8 billion, more than four times the 4 percent that Congress appropriated.

Amid such blatant disregard for the standard of comparability, the more meaningful and basic question in federal pay policy is whether the concept itself should be retained as the theoretical foundation for de- termining federal compensation. Presidents Nixon, Ford, Carter, and Reagan all abandoned the principle of comparability in order to rein in federal deficits. If the case is not made forcefully for the reestablishment of comparability as a guiding principle, this reference point seems certain to lose its relevance to policy decisions in the years ahead.

The concept of comparability is subject to several fundamental criti- cisms which call into question its appropriateness as a guiding principle.

It causes federal pay to lag behind the private sector, and eschews any role for government as a wage leader actively promoting more equitable levels of compensation. More importantly, comparability may sanction wage inequities already present in the private sector, perpetuating sex, race, or ethnic biases and failing to ensure that wage levels are linked to an employee's "comparable worth." For these reasons, it is not obvious that the private sector labor market, with its well-documented shortcomings, provides the best guide for federal wage policies.

The technical problems of implementing comparability also point to more basic conceptual problems worthy of examination. Comparability implicitly assumes that positions in the federal work force are equivalent in most respects to those in the private economy; in fact, this assumption may be unfounded. The size of firms, levels of unionization, historic patterns of wages, degree of specialization, and demographic characteristics of the work force, including age, experience, and education, all may distort comparability assessments or make accurate matching of federal and private sector jobs impossible. Both labor and management have recognized the importance of these variables, particularly in the blue collar pay system, and by negotiating over the industries, firms, and jobs to be surveyed they have engaged in de facto bargaining over wage outcomes. The comparisons between federal and private sector employment are extremely complex, and this reality limits the usefulness of the comparability principle itself.

More exhaustive methodological techniques for calculating comparability offer a poor solution to these problems. A 1975 Rockefeller report on federal pay concluded that decreasing the minimum size of firms would help to eliminate a criticism of bias resulting from the exclusion of smaller firms from the PATC survey. The report questioned, however, whether inclusion of smaller employers would be worth the effort, suggesting that "as earlier field tests and survey experience have demonstrated, this alternative would expend disproportionate amounts of resources for relatively few job matches, possibly without significant effect on pay rates."[15] The panel also noted the increased paper work burden sure to be imposed on the small firms to be included if the survey was widened. The development of a fully accurate survey would be prohibitively expensive, and would not resolve conceptual issues of whether or not large or highly unionized firms are the most appropriate reference point for federal employment.

This recognition of the conceptual shortcomings of the comparability principle is counterbalanced by the awareness that politically acceptable and administratively viable options are not readily available. Lawmakers are uncomfortable with the idea of making the government a wage leader, preferring instead to allow market forces to show the way. Quantifying the differences between public and private sector employment and labor markets would also be extremely difficult, given the broad range of private sector compensation plans and the variation in the degree of security in each job.

An alternative approach would be to pay going market wage rates, unencumbered by administrative machinery. This approach would negate the single national scale now paid to white collar employees, since an acceptable wage in Dry Gulch would not attract a comparable employee in Dallas or Detroit. While the idea of matching private sector local pay scales has much to say for it, its practicality depends to a large extent upon the kind of labor market faced by the federal government. If people are indifferent to the trade off between salary and the benefits of government service versus those of private firms, then the going market wage will attract an adequate number of applicants. If, however, enough potential applicants prefer government employment, for whatever attractions it may offer, then market wage will be too high. On the other hand, if too few would be willing to put up with government bureaucracy, attacks in the media and from politicians, and ever-changing public priorities, then the market wage will be too low.

The option of determining wages by collective bargaining does not appear feasible because of congressional concern that federal managers would "give away the store." Experience with the implementation of the comparability concept does not allow for much optimism that the president and Congress would follow the recommendations of an independent entity no matter how wise and fair its recommendations may be. The government seems, therefore, to resolve the challenge by muddling, no matter what the price is in terms of its impact upon the morale and efficiency of federal employees.

6

Fair Pay and an Efficient Work Force

The comparability principle was originally conceived as a standard of "fair pay," providing an objective basis for defending federal pay levels to taxpayers and workers alike. This frame of reference offered important advantages, for the belief that federal employees were paid what they could earn in the private sector added an essential measure of stability to federal labor-management relations. Denied the right to bargain over wages, federal workers regarded pay systems based on comparability as a guarantee of sharing in the average wage gains of their private sector counterparts. The attempt to establish independent arrangements for adjusting compensation in this manner symbolized a commitment both to equitable treatment of workers and to the maintenance of an efficient work force within the federal establishment.

Despite these laudable goals, increasing disregard of the comparability principle by political leaders has undermined the credibility of such assurances of fair pay. Because political pressures for reduced federal outlays could not be factored into the comparability equation, the determination of federal pay has been forced back into political arenas. Perceptions regarding the comparability of public and private sector wages continue to have a major impact on worker attitudes and demands, but expectations that federal compensation will be adjusted in any predictable or independent fashion have been frustrated. Federal unions have little choice but to return to political lobbying as a means of securing equitable pay on behalf of their members.

The virtual abandonment of pay systems based on comparability resurrects the central issue of compensation which is to avoid over-compensation of federal employees while ensuring pay adequate to preserve an efficient work force. This balance can be assessed directly by using data on private sector wages to determine whether federal workers are overpaid, or indirectly by examining job turnover trends, strike threats, and other possible indicators of inadequate compensation. While such evidence seldom is conclusive, it can suggest directions for future reform efforts to replace the faltering comparability systems.

Are Federal Workers Overpaid?

The comparability calculations discussed earlier provide one basis for considering whether federal workers are overpaid. Repeated recommendations of advisory committees in favor of large increases in federal pay indicate that the wages of federal workers have fallen behind their private sector counterparts, and that the former are not overpaid in comparison to the latter. Of course, estimates of total comparability are considerably more tenuous, and have rendered no clear verdict on the relative compensation of federal and private sector employees. Moreover, comparability studies are based on national averages and, therefore, may not reflect conditions in specific labor markets.

Yet critics of the comparability principle abound arguing that, whatever the facts may be, the generally negative public image of federal bureaucrats, nourished by the media and more recently by the Reagan administration, has ensured added credence to analyses concluding that federal workers are paid too generously.

Early comparisons of compensation levels in public and private sectors focused on the identification of similar jobs in each sector.[1] These studies concluded that federal workers were overpaid, especially at the lower end of the pay scale. However, the failure of the studies to account for differences in age, experience, and other employee characteristics limited the usefulness of their findings. Later efforts overcompensated for these shortcomings emphasizing disparities in the compensation of employees with equivalent skills and personal characteristics, regardless of their jobs. This methodology does not provide direct guidance for comparability calculations under current law, which mandates comparisons between similar jobs rather than similar employees, but it does shed some light on the question of whether federal workers are paid more than their value in the private labor market.

Several studies have found that federal pay is higher than could be justified by reference to the unique characteristics of the federal work force alone. One such study found that at least 30 percent of the differential between workers with equal personal characteristics such as age, sex, race, experience, and education could not be explained except by the fact that federal workers were overpaid.[2] Another study using the same methodology compared a sample of older workers in an attempt to more carefully define variables such as education and experience and to narrow the discrepancies in such characteristics.[3] The average hourly wage rate in the private sector was, according to this study, one-third lower than the average federal rate. It was estimated that if equal returns to workers with the same personal characteristics were the rule in both sectors, the federal average wage rate for the groups studied would have been $3.95. This type of analysis is not without its shortcomings. Statisticians frequently disagree as to which variables should be considered in the calculation of average wages or even how each variable should be defined.[4] Finally, the difficulty of obtaining comparable data cannot be ignored.

A more recent review of federal pay attempted to gauge the extent of oversupply of workers for federal jobs by using job turnover data as a proxy.[5] This indirect approach, which implicitly accounts for fringe benefits ignored by direct wage comparisons, resulted in the finding that federal workers were 7.3 percent less likely to leave their jobs than workers in the private sector. Yet, as the author indicated, job turnover is hardly an ideal surrogate for labor supply data, and the turnover figures themselves failed to distinguish between layoffs and voluntary quits.

Given inevitable methodological and conceptual problems and the paucity of comparable data, a definitive answer to the question of whether federal workers are overpaid may not be obtainable. Nevertheless, even crude comparisons of 1981 wage data (excluding fringe benefits) in various labor markets across the country suggest that the popular notion of federal employees receiving excessive compensation, if ever valid, may no longer apply (Tables 8 and 9). Following several years of pay caps, repeated departures from the comparability principle, and costly indexed early retirements, rough comparisons indicate that it is time to at least take a fresh look at the federal pay issue.

Table 8 compares federal and private pay for ten blue collar occupations in seven wage areas. The federal data for blue collar pay scales are from the wage survey conducted in each area according to the rules specified in the law and the limiting criteria imposed administratively. The private sector data are from the Bureau of Labor Statistics annual surveys of the same wage areas. While the lowest skill occupation in each area is better paid in the federal sector in every case, a review of the pay for the other nine occupations shows that this is not a pattern. Of the 68 comparisons, federal employees came out ahead in 28 (41 percent) instances.

These blue collar contrasts must be viewed with caution. The average wage rates for the private sector reflect seniority, whereas the federal rate shown is fixed at the second step of each grade. The average federal wage may be slightly above or below this second step rate, depending upon the longevity of the work force in any given grade. Secondly, there are several months' difference in almost all of the comparison dates, and this time lag will inevitably work to the advantage of one sector or the other. Still, the comparison does suggest that on the average federal rates in 1981 were comparable to those in the private sector, although wide differentials existed within local areas, which were presumably the basis for comparisons.

A similar comparison for white collar workers in ten occupations nationally and in seven cities around the country also strongly suggests that federal employees do not uniformly earn more than their counterparts (Table 9). Of the seventy-four comparisons made, they came out ahead of their private sector counterparts in seventeen instances, or in about 23 percent of these cases. Some of the shortcomings of the blue collar comparisons are evident in this white collar data as well, although both federal and private sector data in this case reflect average wage rates rather than step pay. In addition, variations in the seniority of respective work forces and time lags between the PATC and other BLS surveys have the potential for skewing wage comparisons. These qualifications do not seem so overriding as to eliminate the usefulness of this kind of comparison.

While the randomly selected wage areas do not constitute a "scientific" study, or offer a basis for policy formulation, the data suggest little evidence for concluding that federal pay in 1981 was higher than private pay for comparable jobs. Moreover, only white collar jobs in the seven lower federal groups were included in the comparison. As shown

Table 8. A 1981 comparison of federal and private hourly wage rates for selected blue collar occupations in seven cities did not disclose any patterns*

Occupation	Milwaukee Federal	Milwaukee Private	Atlanta Federal	Atlanta Private	New York City Federal	New York City Private	Cleveland Federal	Cleveland Private	Omaha Federal	Omaha Private	San Antonio Federal	San Antonio Private	San Francisco Federal	San Francisco Private
Janitor	7.10	4.96	5.49	3.94	6.49	6.17	7.01	6.22	6.13	4.26	5.10	3.68	7.43	7.09
Material handler	7.61	8.88	6.09	7.62	6.86	8.14	7.41	9.31	6.48	7.31	5.43	4.80	7.88	8.79
Packer	8.33	7.12	7.26	4.99	7.58	5.89	8.57	7.85	6.95	7.07	6.13	4.10	8.77	9.40
Warehouseman	8.71	8.03	7.83	8.56	7.93	6.95	8.51	7.49	7.26	7.73	6.48	5.10	9.23	9.31
Forklift operator	8.71	8.76	7.83	7.82	7.93	7.49	8.51	9.45	7.26	8.26	6.48	5.57	9.23	9.46
Truckdriver (medium)	9.05	8.75	8.36	7.48	8.30	9.41	8.25	10.44	7.51	9.32	6.84	7.64	9.68	11.17
Truckdriver (heavy)	9.38	10.52	8.91	6.68	8.66	10.43	9.26	8.85	7.76	10.22	—	4.81	10.13	11.89
Carpenter	10.08	10.99	9.99	9.41	9.38	8.83	10.02	11.79	8.25	7.64	8.15	—	11.02	11.39
Electrician	10.41	11.93	10.53	10.83	9.75	10.23	10.34	11.90	8.50	10.06	8.59	8.81	11.47	11.95
Automotive mechanic	10.41	10.99	10.53	10.62	9.75	10.57	10.34	10.93	8.50	9.98	8.59	7.73	11.47	12.84

Sources: Office of Personnel Management; and Bureau of Labor Statistics *Area Wage Survey* in each area.
*Federal wages shown are those for the second step of each grade. Private sector wages are BLS averages for each area. The dates surveys were taken varied.

Table 9. A 1981 comparison of federal and private annual salaries for selected white collar occupations nationally and in 7 cities did not indicate any patterns

GS Grade	Occupation	Federal	Private	Cleveland	Milwaukee	Oklahoma City	Omaha	San Antonio	Atlanta	New York City
1	File Clerk I	8,070	8,420	8,220	9,130	8,190	—	7,490	8,080	8,270
2	Accounting Clerk I	9,150	9,580	10,840	10,120	11,910	—	—	11,180	9,850
3	Stenographer I	10,440	13,190	14,920	11,830	—	12,840	12,950	14,510	11,860
4	Secretary I	12,150	12,450	12,460	13,860	12,640	—	10,010	11,730	12,300
4	Computer Operator I	12,160	10,870	11,440	13,050	11,670	14,200	9,280	13,810	12,530
5	Drafter IV	13,880	19,340	18,800	17,810	16,820	17,600	15,420	17,760	17,370
5	Accounting Clerk IV	13,880	16,890	16,350	14,530	18,360	15,260	13,360	14,430	13,390
6	Computer Operator III	15,700	14,650	17,750	17,840	17,210	16,870	13,600	19,990	17,600
7	Drafter V	17,180	24,130	21,870	20,230	20,180	19,760	—	21,920	20,540
8	Secretary V	19,520	19,620	19,240	17,530	16,020	18,820	16,090	19,680	18,950

Sources: Bureau of Labor Statistics, National Survey of Professional, Administrative, Technical, and Clerical Pay, March 1981 (Washington: Government Printing Office, September 1981), pp. 73-74 (columns 2 and 3); and Bureau of Labor Statistics, *Area Wage Survey* for each area listed (Washington: Government Printing Office, 1981). The dates surveys were taken varied.

earlier (Figure 5) the higher federal grades have lagged more than the lower grades in the 1981 comparability survey.

Pay Freezes and Poor Morale

For those employees at the top end of the federal pay scale, at least, indirect evidence of inadequate compensation may provide clearer insights than direct salary and fringe benefits studies. Even as the debate over absolute comparisons between federal and private sector pay continues, it is generally acknowledged that the federal pay scale is compressed.[6] Thus, while overall job turnover rates in the federal sector may not reveal any surprises, a closer examination of retirement patterns and voluntary departures among personnel in upper levels suggests that federal pay in these ranks may not be high enough, or that fully indexed retirement benefits are too generous, to maintain staff morale or to retain qualified senior executives in the federal government.

The potential dangers of underpaying top executives in the civil service were acknowledged and addressed in the 1978 reform legislation promoted by the Carter administration. Attempting to resolve problems of inadequate pay while also adding a measure of flexibility to a system Carter viewed as rigid and ossified, the Civil Service Reform Act created the Senior Executive Service (SES). It was to be composed of top-level employees who were willing to trade some employment security for a chance of greater financial reward. The hope was that the SES would attract and retain qualified managers in the top three grades of the personnel classification system while also allowing the "deadwood" to be weeded from these highest ranks. Although joining the system was optional for those already on the civil service rolls, more than 90 percent of the then eligible "super grade" managers opted to join.

If evaluated in terms of its success in alleviating perceived pay problems among top level managers, the SES has neither fulfilled promises nor met expectations. Between 1977 and 1981, legislation tying the pay of top federal executives to congressional salaries effectively froze compensation for career executives and blocked SES pay raises. Faced with the perennial political liabilities of legislating their own pay hikes, members of Congress repeatedly refused either to increase their own salaries or to lift the pay ceiling that this freeze created for top level executives. As one official noted: "It doesn't sell too well in Broken Bow, Oklahoma, when someone making $50,000 a year is voted a taxpayer-financed raise."[7] In 1981 Congress found a way to raise at least temporarily members' real take-home pay by increasing their tax exempt expense allowances without raising formal annual pay. This compassion was confined to members of Congress, however, offering no relief to the top hired hands in the executive branch. In response to public criticism, even the Congress was forced to give up the special treatment.

Between 1969 and October 1981 the consumer price index rose 156 percent, whereas SES salaries rose only 43 percent. The dissatisfaction engendered by this inequity led to increasing attempts to use political pressure to secure a pay raise in 1981. In September the Reagan administration partially acceded to these demands and favored a raise for the SES equal to the 4.8 percent raise allowed the rest of the work force. The GAO, however, strongly endorsed a 14.7 percent raise arguing that "raising the pay cap to $57,500 would be cost effective. . . . Granting the raise would reduce Federal outlays for the first 3 years because executives at the pay cap would not retire and replacement salary costs would be avoided."[8] The GAO view prevailed, but not without some effective lobbying. Congress accepted the GAO recommendation and lifted the pay cap to $57,500.

The December 1981 increase in the pay ceiling only offered a brief respite for federal executives, in that the cap was retained and inflation continues to erode their salaries with no immediate prospect for periodic adjustment. The Civil Service Reform Act sought to compensate senior federal executives for lack of comparability raises through a new bonus system, in which monetary awards would be tied to annual performance appraisals. Without question, much of the emphasis of the reform legislation was to spur bureaucratic efficiency, in the hope that a motivated managerial elite would evoke greater effort from subordinates and create a ripple effect throughout the civil service. The principle may be sound, but it has been no substitute for assurances of fair pay.

The bonus system originally was to reward as many as half of all senior executives with either presidential awards of $20,000 for distinguished service, merit awards of $10,000, or performance awards of up to 20 percent of base pay. Since the original act, however, Congress has reduced the number of executives eligible to receive such awards from 50 to 25 percent, and OPM further limited the awards to 20 percent of those eligible. This action caused so much consternation that the Senior Executives Association (SEA) has filed suit against OPM for violating the Civil Service Reform Act by administratively limiting the awards. Congress came to the rescue of OPM and included the 20 percent limitation as part of the 1981 Reconciliation Act. Even the lifting of the pay cap did not mollify the SEA. It contends that the entire senior service was built upon the exchange of job security for performance awards, and that to subject executives to the first without the second is in violation of the law.

In addition to these restrictions on access to executive bonuses, the broader impact of such awards on pay has been limited by their disproportionate concentration within the very highest grades. The skewed distribution of awards may reflect the greater visibility of top executives or may be intended to offset the pay cap which has eliminated pay differentials between the highest grades. In either case, in 1980 the officials in the top two (out of six) grades accounted for 14 percent of the total SES strength but received 29 percent of all bonuses, while the 17 percent in the bottom two grades received 6 percent of all bonuses.

Finally, it has been charged that the boards responsible for appraisal have not properly measured performance, and that political appointees have ignored those evaluations in making bonus awards. Employees need to know what is expected of them. As one report argued, "Even employees whose jobs require a high degree of self-direction or who are personally inclined to define their own work responsibility require definition of their objectives and the standards by which their work will be evaluated."[9] In the absence of clear performance standards, the new appraisal system has fostered the widespread perception among SES members that the system is unfair and rigged.

Following three years of sporadic administration of this system of bonus awards, complaints regarding the government's failure to deliver promised rewards to members of the Senior Executive Service abound. Anecdotes of rock bottom morale are buttressed by statistics showing a dramatic increase in the number of executives retiring from the service. A study of 1,000 SES members in April 1981 by the Merit Systems Protection Board found that one of every four planned to leave within two years, even though many were not eligible for retirement pay upon resignation.[10] Clearly, "experience drain" remains a significant problem.

Feeding this resentment has been the lack of flexibility in careers and management action that was to replace old rigidities. In the spring of 1981 the Federal Executive Institute (a training organization for senior executives) surveyed its graduates and found that more than half were of the opinion that the SES hindered federal management effectiveness.

Movement in and out of agencies seems to be about the same as in the past, and many argue that the SES has made no difference in this regard. And while pay has not met expectations, the loss of job security is acutely felt by members of the SES.[11]

Middle management employees apparently fared better than the top supervisors. In an attempt to increase productivity among supervisors and middle-level managers at the GS-13, 14, and 15 levels (just below the SES) with salaries ranging from $33,586 to the cap of $50,112 as of mid-1982, the 1978 law replaced step increases based on longevity with a system tied to merit. While in-grade increases had been theoretically based on merit, some 98 percent of those eligible received them regularly. The 1978 law eliminated longevity (in-grade) increases, and guaranteed only half the usual annual comparability raise for those in the three middle management grades. Under the new law, the extra funds from annual raises that would have gone for longevity increases are pooled, and supervisors now compete for that pool of funds on the basis of performance.

Initial attacks on the system seem to reflect more fear of change than disapproval of results. One writer has commented that in the federal establishment "half the people are confused by [merit pay], the other half are terrified by it."[12] Early returns do not indicate much cause for alarm.

Some studies suggest that though there is indeed concern with the merit pay system, managers trust their superiors and coworkers enough that they are willing to give it a try.[13] Others have found that federal managers remain leery of the system.[14] There has been enough dissatisfaction to prompt one congressman representing a large number of federal workers to introduce legislation to end the merit pay system and revert to allowing managers the same percentage increase as all other white collar employees plus merit bonuses when appropriate. Yet it is hard to avoid the conclusion that the merit pay system does not deserve the brunt of such criticism. It is the pay ceiling that continues to be the source of distortions in compensation and disruption of rational incentive systems in the federal establishment.

No doubt, there are reasons for poor morale among top executives and middle managers other than shabby pay treatment. Upper-level federal employees face many obstacles and potential sources of frustration which private sector managers never confront. In addition to encountering conflict with political appointees top federal managers have only limited control (within the constraints of the civil service system) over workers beneath them, and they are regularly placed in the middle of political battles between powerful interest groups which the Congress "delegates" to the executive branch rather than resolving itself. Federal managers must respond not only to Congress whose members are far more sensitive to pressures from their constituencies in the electorate than to the needs of personnel or program managers, but also to political appointees with little knowledge of the programs and with extremely short terms in office. Finally, federal executives and supervisors seldom have a concrete bottom line by which to measure their success, and all too often find their performance contrasted with rhetorical ideals of legislation which bear little relationship to attainable goals.

These nonwage related problems contribute to the perception that public managers are less content with their roles than their private sector counterparts. One comparative study of top managerial attitudes found that job satisfaction of private sector executives grows with age and experience, while the job satisfaction of a public administrator diminishes with experience.[15] It seems significant, however, that another survey of federal managers found 91 percent enjoyed the work they performed, and that their frustrations came from other aspects of federal employment—including lack of appreciation and low pay.[16]

If the increases in membership in protective associations such as the Federal Managers Association (about 15,000 members) or the Senior Executives Association (1,300 members) are any guide, top officials are becoming more active in attempts to improve conditions in the federal establishment. They will certainly find the politics of federal pay difficult, and yet the government can ill afford the mass exodus of experienced and talented managers who administer federal programs that account for more than a fifth of the national product. More adequate compensation, more strongly linking merit, performance, and financial rewards, is long overdue and will go a long way toward alleviating frustrations in the bureaucracy's highest ranks.

Other Signs of Discontent

The exodus of competent managers must be viewed as a strong indication of dissatisfaction with pay and other elements of federal employment within the upper, nonunionized grades of the civil service. Private sector parallels suggest that similar discontent in nonmanagerial ranks,

Table 10. **Work stoppages in government, 1960-80**

Year	Federal government		State government		Local government	
	Stoppages	Workers*	Stoppages	Workers*	Stoppages	Workers*
1960-1969	10	6.5	85	40.9	1097	657.4
1970-1979	12	163.0	352	288.3	3866	1651.3
1980	1	.9	45	10.0	493	212.7

Source: Bureau of Labor Statistics, "Work Stoppages in Government, 1942-1980," *Government Employee Relations Report* Reference File (Washington: Bureau of National Affairs, 1982), p. 71:1014; see note 17 for a more recent study that lists 39 strikes.
*In thousands.

if it exists, would be expressed more directly through the actions of federal employee unions. Yet federal unions have seldom displayed signs of militancy and they have been more reluctant to press their demands in an aggressive manner during recent retrenchments.

Historically, federal workers have not been so prone as other public employees to resort to strikes in voicing their dissatisfaction with pay (Table 10). Federal law since the Lloyd-LaFollette Act of 1912 has repeatedly banned strikes by federal employees. The Taft-Hartley Act requires immediate discharge of federal employees who engage in a strike. From 1960 to 1980 federal strikes accounted for less than 1 percent of all government work stoppages, involving 6 percent of all striking government workers. Still between 1962 and 1981 as many as seven strikes involved 1,000 or more employees. The two largest strikes during the period involved 152,000 postal employees in 1970 and 12,500 air traffic controllers in 1981. The provision of the law notwithstanding, the treatment accorded the strikers differed. In fourteen of the thirty-nine strikes listed (including the 1970 postal strike) in the study no penalties were imposed while in eight cases the strikers were discharged.[17]

Yet the official statistics contain many flaws. For one thing, data gathering has been dependent upon newspaper accounts of strikes rather than systematic reports by either agencies or unions. In addition, the BLS definition of a strike is confined to cases where employees are absent for an entire shift. Preliminary and as yet unpublished findings of a study sponsored by the House Post Office and Civil Service Committee suggest numerous small and unreported job actions by federal employees over almost every aspect of employment, including compensation. Still, federal employees are less prone to strike or slowdown than are either private sector or other government workers.

The disparity between federal and other public sector work stoppages is not solely due to the federal ban on strikes. As late as 1969 no public employee strikes were permitted at any level of government, although since then nine states and the Virgin Islands have granted limited rights to strike to state and local employees. Yet even during the period of prohibition, lower-level government workers conducted numerous work stoppages.

A number of explanations have been offered for the relative lack of militancy in the federal sector. Strikes by federal employees are more visible than those conducted by state and local employees or private sector workers. It may also be easier for employees to take on local or state governments than it is to challenge the might of the federal government. Another possibility is that other government and private sector workers find strikes more meaningful because they enjoy the right to negotiate over wages. From the mid-1800s to 1960, the relatively few officially recognized federal strikes involved wage issues, although at times they focused on demands for reducing work hours as an indirect way of negotiating wages.

Perhaps the most persuasive account of the relative lack of militancy among federal unions is that they have precious little to bargain over. Strikes are most useful as a source of leverage and pressure in negotiations and as an alternative if bargaining fails. Labor relations in the federal government have developed into a system in which political action has outweighed negotiation as a means of achieving desired ends, thus making the strike an inappropriate weapon for federal employees. When one is engaged in political bargaining, withdrawing from the field of action generally does not serve one's cause, but rather alienates political leaders and stiffens opposition. Even today, most federal union leaders remain lobbyists, not bargainers.

Since the enactment of the 1978 civil service reform law, federal unions have resorted increasingly to "back door" approaches to circumvent the prohibition against bargaining over wages. These attempts, although of questionable legal status, typically have taken the form of arbitration disputes governing classifications, overtime, shift differentials, and back pay. On occasion, however, militant unions have adopted a more direct, combative posture in voicing their dissatisfaction with federal pay and other nonbargainable working conditions as in the Professional Air Traffic Controllers Organization (PATCO) effort to expand negotiable issues in 1981. The results of this strike are not likely to encourage militancy of federal unions. Still the PATCO struggle is worthy of examination as an indication of what may lie ahead for federal unions.

The 15,000 air traffic controllers union was not the prototype of a typical federal union. It had succeeded in organizing nearly 90 percent of the eligible employees, possibly the highest membership/representation ratio among federal unions. PATCO was also among the few unions whose dedication to collective bargaining exceeded its reliance on the political system. Although it occasionally went to Congress to pursue its objectives, it often resorted to tactics long familiar to private sector unions.

The work conditions of air traffic controllers were also relatively unique, contributing both to PATCO's strength and to generally poor labor relations in the air traffic control system since the early 1960s. Rising airport congestion, an impersonal emphasis on technology rather than worker skills, and a rigid, order-giving mentality among air traffic supervisors with military backgrounds have all been cited as causes of tension, dissatisfaction, and, indirectly, of PATCO's growing militancy.[18] In 1970, when public attention was focused on striking postal workers, PATCO staged a "sick out" in order to get more controllers and better equipment. Management, unable to procure these things from the Congress, not so subtly encouraged the strike. Organized actions, though on a smaller scale, occurred again in 1976 and in 1978. Each new concerted use of power encouraged union leaders and brought members closer together as a group.

Discontent finally boiled over in the union's 1980-81 round of bargaining with the Federal Aviation Administration (FAA). Confident of its ability to cripple the air traffic system, PATCO demanded that the FAA support a bill before Congress that would have granted controllers an immediate annual $10,000 raise, and a reduction in the work week from forty hours to thirty-two. (Base pay for controllers was $20,500 and ranged up to nearly $50,000 at some of the busiest airports.) Surprisingly, this proposal was not only given serious consideration but was actually accepted in limited form. The FAA, faced with a strike deadline which they had every reason to believe was genuine, bargained with PATCO over wages.

As a result of PATCO's tough bargaining stance, the agency officials signed a contract with union negotiators on June 22, 1981, which obliged the administration to seek legislative approval of some $40 million in

101

new benefits, including: an average raise of $2,300 a year (a 6.6 percent increase on top of the 4.8 percent expected for other federal workers); forty-two hours of pay for a forty-hour work week; elimination of the overall total salary ceiling on premium pay for overtime; an increase in the night differential from 10 to 15 percent; and provision of a retraining allowance for controllers with five years consecutive service who sought to qualify for other jobs. Not since the 1970 postal strike had anything similar been attempted by a federal union. Yet the controllers felt that they were being shortchanged, and voted down this agreement by over 95 percent.

Upon returning to the bargaining table, Robert Poli, president of the union, imposed another strike deadline only three days away. When the government refused to budge, the union defied an injunction imposed in 1970 and applied in mid-1978 by a U.S. district court, and went on strike. Although the resulting disruption was severe for a few days, the airline industry was not substantially damaged. The strikers were replaced by military controllers, supervisors, and nonstriking controllers working extra shifts, who were able to reroute some traffic and keep the system functioning. Despite help from other unions, both in the federal sector and outside it (more than was publicized at the time), air traffic resumed quickly at a reduced level, and the strike was broken when President Reagan fired the controllers en masse and the FLRA decertified PATCO. In July 1982 the union filed for bankruptcy, essentially marking its end as an organization.

Very few federal unions have PATCO's background of high membership, militancy, and experience with slowdowns and other concerted action. The consent of the FAA to recommend to Congress a contract comprised of wage items was precedent-setting, but is not likely to be repeated in the foreseeable future by other agencies. However, if current erosion of job security, pay freezes, and other cutbacks drive more federal workers into unions, the latter may be driven to more traditional forms of union protest. Whatever the cause of quiescence in the past, it seems at least plausible that signs of discontent from the rank and file will grow to match the already visible dissatisfaction of management personnel in the federal government.

Aside from the need of defining the scope of collective bargaining, a more activist role with added powers for the impasses panel is also in order as long as federal employees are denied the right to use the ultimate pressure in resolving differences with management. Included in the added authority of the panel would be the power to rule on issues that unions cannot bring formally to the bargaining table. The current system limits sharply the jurisdiction of the impasses panel and consequently prevents the panel from intervening in many disputes. Several proposals that would broaden the scope of the FSIP have surfaced. FLRA chairman Ronald Haughton, an experienced mediator and arbitrator, has recommended a public procedure that would bring the parties together and require them to "show cause" why they have come to an impasse and why the union wishes to strike. He contends that the public hearing would serve an important function by allowing both labor and management to air their differences in a public forum before neutrals and might suffice to bring both sides into line.[19]

Other changes may also be necessary. One might be to allow the panel to intervene by imposing specific contract language on the parties, as it is now authorized to do in cases involving narrowly confined collective bargaining issues. The arrangements might take the form attempted in the controllers' first contract with the FAA (which was rejected by the union), binding management to advocate the agreed upon package of wages and fringe benefits before the Congress. This requirement upon management would not constitute a final wage settlement, and the Congress would still have to decide whether to accept the negotiated package or to send management back to the bargaining table. The onus for this decision, however, would rest squarely on the shoulders of Congress.

Prospects for Reform

If one accepts the premise that the present system for determining federal compensation does not guarantee federal workers fair and adequate pay, and that in at least some instances federal wages have fallen considerably short of pay levels for selected occupations, or areas, the question becomes one of how to reshape existing pay systems to better serve the interests of labor, management, and the taxpayer. A review of basic reform proposals regarding federal pay is useful in summarizing the preceding discussion.

The comparability system has not worked as an independent mechanism for setting federal pay primarily because its rationale has proven less compelling than short-term political pressures. As along as the federal policymakers can promulgate alternative pay plans with relative ease, it seems likely that such "self-adjusting" pay systems will be circumvented out of political expedience. With the exception of a handful of representatives with large numbers of federal workers in their districts, members of Congress find little to be gained in supporting pay increases for federal employees with an unmistakably negative, if unjustified, public image.

Even if the comparability principle was allowed to have a binding effect on federal compensation, the insistence on placing general schedule employees throughout the country on a single wage scale conflicts with the goal of paying workers what they could otherwise earn in the private sector. For this reason, the 1975 Rockefeller Commission suggested that the general schedule be replaced by two separate pay groups: clerical and technical employees would be paid prevailing rates in their locality, as are blue collar workers, while executives and professionals, who frequently compete for jobs in a national labor market, would remain on a single pay schedule. This revised structure would more accurately reflect the types of labor market in which the two groups operate, and would avoid large disparities between federal and private sector wages for clerical and technical employees in areas where prevailing wages deviate sharply from the national average.

Most federal unions have opposed and continue to resist this type of pay reform. The initial reaction of the American Federation of Government Employees (AFGE) was that the implementation of the proposal would create a "caste or elitist system" and that the union was "unalterably opposed to the proposal."[20] More recently the AFGE has apparently relaxed its position on the proposed change. The National Federation of Federal Employees (NFFE) claimed the proposal was "counter to the pay trend . . . in that the movement is toward a single national rate. The administration of special occupational schedules would be the cause of irrational internal alignment and tend to 'undemocratize' the system."[21] At least partially as a result of union opposition, the Congress has not actively considered the Rockefeller Commission's recommendation.

The concept of setting wage rates for some portion of the federal work force on a local basis touches upon the more basic issue of whether federal employees finally should be granted the right to bargain over wages. The division of federal workers into three major salary groups (blue collar, clerical/technical, and executive/professional) might offer the best method of introducing collective bargaining into the federal government for two of the three pay groups accounting for the bulk of federal employees. (Management officials, presumably to be included in the third pay group, are not eligible for union representation.) Private and many state and local government employees already enjoy access to such negotiation processes, and equity suggests that federal employees are due the same rights. The shifts to local wage determination could provide an opportunity for a smooth transition to wage negotiation in the federal establishment.

One of the central arguments presented in opposition to wage negotiation on this local basis has been that the lack of profit consideration would allow unions to gain disproportionate pay increases, and that such increases would disrupt congressional control over expenditures. It is not clear, however, that local bargaining over wages would automatically result in higher pay scales than those recommended through the supposedly objective comparability approach. The precedent of wage bargaining in state and local governments is particularly relevant in this regard.

The experience of the states in which employees have the right to bargain over wages, including nine that grant a limited right to strike, suggests that unions do not raise public sector wages beyond those of the private sector. Although unions certainly act to raise salary levels beyond what they might have been absent a union, it appears that competitive market forces and the fiscal position of the public treasury are more crucial to wage scales than the limited power of unions.[22]

There is little reason to believe that localized bargaining of federal employees would raise the wage scales significantly above the prevailing union rates in their communities, although one could expect that they would act to keep wages from falling *below* this level. From 1970-1981, when federal unions were indirectly bargaining over wages locally, the average hourly rate of federal blue collar (FWS) employees rose 136 percent compared with the 120 percent wage gain for private sector nonsupervisory employees. These data would suggest that there is need to monitor closely local wage bargaining, but they also indicate that concern over runaway increases is not justified.

In the fiscal 1982 budget, the civilian employee wage and fringe benefits bill for the estimated 2.1 million executive branch employees was $60 billion, accounting for about 8 percent of total federal outlays. It is undoubtedly true that there would be some loss of control over this item in the federal budget if a system of local wage negotiations was adopted.

Yet the Congress has managed to find ways of dealing with entitlement programs obligating more than five times the outlay that federal salaries require, and legislative oversight of bargaining ground rules and the power to disapprove contracts signed by agencies would provide the necessary controls over excessive raises.

This revised pay structure could offer important advantages for management as well. Negotiation on a local basis would allow agency officials to include trade offs between higher wages and greater management freedom to fire unproductive employees. More important, the principle of equity might be better served by the increased flexibility of local wage determination. Instead of determining wage adjustments on the basis of national trends, which are frequently of doubtful relevance, federal pay would be responsive to local conditions.

The assumption that there would be no check on the outcome reached from local bargaining instead of on Capitol Hill has been based on pure speculation. Imaginative approaches can be developed to balance the rights of federal workers, the management needs of the government, and the constitutional mandates prescribing the limits of executive action. Modified forms of binding arbitration would allow the impasses panel to settle labor-management differences. The government would retain significant clout in its power to contract out functions to the private sector, and in the final analysis Congress would retain the power to reject negotiated agreements. Mounting frustrations, as evident in the PATCO strike, could be dissipated.

It is difficult to argue that the current pay system in which unions, denied direct input, must "bargain" through political channels on Capitol Hill and in the White House is fairer or more efficient than a collective bargaining process similar to that found working effectively in the private sector. The unique nature of the federal sector cannot be ignored, and modified bargaining arrangements are warranted in this regard. At present, it seems highly unlikely that this kind of system will be enacted in the near future. Yet the existing comparability system is clearly faltering, if it still exists at all, and the time has come to extend the bargaining rights enjoyed by employees in the private sector to federal workers and their unions.

7

A Return to the Spoils System?

The past two decades in federal employee relations have been characterized by significant gains in rights of workers to be represented by unions of their choice. Increasing numbers of federal employees are now represented by unions who have fostered the gradual expansion of collective bargaining and sought to protect the individual rights of their members. Civil servants now can pursue their grievances through either statutory or negotiated procedures, and they are more able than ever before to influence the conditions of their employment at the bargaining table. Even in the area of pay, which unions are prevented from addressing directly through negotiations, federal workers have succeeded in promoting a heightened awareness of how their wages compare with those of their counterparts in the private sector and indirectly to affect pay issues.

This pattern of continuing advances is threatened by indications that the Reagan administration may be preparing to back away from some fundamental tenets of the civil service system. The principles of merit and job security which insulate the civil service from political manipulation have proven to be troublesome obstacles in the ideological drive to reduce federal spending and to ensure less active government roles. Merit hiring procedures have limited the ability of the administration to strengthen political loyalty within federal agencies, and civil service regulations governing firings and layoffs have hindered proposed reductions in force (RIFs). These tensions between managerial discretion and civil service protections occur in virtually every administration, yet the current one seems prepared to press these concerns further and harder than ever before.

Worker Protection versus Political Responsiveness

The effectiveness of a civil service structure depends on achieving an acceptable balance between goals of protecting workers from political manipulation and maintaining political responsiveness within the broader system. The civil service traces its origins to 1883 when it was established as a reaction to the perceived excesses of the spoils system which controlled the hiring and firing of federal employees. The system was not intended to tie the hands of the chief executive, and retained his power to appoint top personnel to preserve the bureaucracy's responsiveness to political direction from above. Given this delicate balancing act between the political authorities and individual rights, control over the actions and status of civil servants could be exercised only within a relatively rigid institutional framework of personnel regulations and procedures. It was hoped that this balance would nurture a federal work force that was competent and yet still manageable by political leaders.

Before the institution of civil service guarantees of job security and merit hiring, the political devotion of federal employees to the president had a much greater bearing on their length of service than did their competence. With frequent changes in administration, federal workers seldom gained the experience of lengthy tenure and were distinguished primarily by unwavering allegiance to the executive branch of the government rather than by their professional talents. As the administrative responsibilities of government grew more complex the need for a professional and stable work force could not be ignored. An independent civil service was conceived as a means of breaking the iron link between political loyalty and federal employment, thereby providing the element of continuity necessary to sustain a competent federal work force.

In this context, worker rights under civil service statutes were steadily strengthened and centralized until the mid-1970s. Periodic attempts by administrations to circumvent personnel regulations during the post-World War II era fueled the trend toward more rigid procedures in federal employee relations. For example, revelations in the early 1970s that the White House personnel office had circulated a manual for trusted agency heads instructing them how to exploit loopholes in hiring and firing regulations caused the Civil Service Commission to tighten its central control of personnel regulations.[1] Such lengths in attempts to neutralize "disloyal" employees have been rare, indeed, but every incoming administration has voiced concern that civil service rules would prevent it from carrying out its political mandate.

When President Carter made civil service reform legislation a top priority of his administration, numerous observers had already expressed concern that the bureaucracy had become too burdened with civil service protections to respond promptly and effectively to any policy directive. A 1978 report by the Committee for Economic Development summarized this view: "[T]he constraints on most governments are unnecessarily paralyzing. Personnel regulations designed to meet the problems of an earlier age are seldom pruned when they have outlived their usefulness. Controls established to guard against political favoritism and graft now pose the equally ominous danger of crippling public-service operations."[2] The consensus that personnel rules had become unduly cumbersome provided the underpinning for the Civil Service Reform Act's effort to bolster government efficiency. By "streamlining" the plethora of civil service regulations, the Carter administration sought to expedite the handling of personnel matters and to provide new incentives for management initiative without undermining basic assurances of job security in the civil service.

The reform act did not make significant departures from the merit principle which provides the foundation for the civil service, and thus has not in itself politicized federal employee relations. Yet the 1978 legislation has not been particularly successful in bolstering the efficiency of government agencies. Federal political managers still rarely enjoy the flexibility to choose their own staffs or the discretion to control and direct their subordinates.

The Office of Personnel Management continues to dictate uniform recruitment and hiring procedures as well as rigid specifications concerning personnel practices. Personnel ceilings and contract/consultant guidelines, imposed by the Office of Management and Budget, further restrict the ability of federal managers to respond to their needs. Amid these restrictions, the debate over the appropriate balance among worker protection, managerial flexibility, and political responsiveness has continued.

To a large extent, cumbersome civil service regulations seem an inevitable response to the unique nature of employee relations in the federal sector. With the president fulfilling dual roles as political leader and chief executive, reasonable checks on political influence are essential for the development of an independent and competent federal work force which can administer national policy in a neutral and professional manner. No doubt a price is paid for the stability and continuity in terms of lost efficiency, and there remains a danger that guarantees of job security could spawn an intransigent work force insulated from the periodically changing management control. The choice cannot be between extremes of complete worker protection and total management prerogatives in hiring and firing, but rather the civil service system must reflect a prudent mixture of the two.

While successive presidents have not sought a return to the fully politicized work force of the 1880s, most have struggled to reconcile the constraints of the civil service system with their own political goals and ideological perceptions. This tension, inherent in the balance between worker protection and political responsiveness, has been reflected in recurring frictions between career civil servants and their politically appointed bosses. The latter, identifying their interests closely with the wishes of the president to whom they owe their positions, tend to view the careerists as bureaucrats whose dedication to self-preservation and protection of turf or agency interests overshadows their sense of broader public responsibility. Career executives, conversely, view political appointees as temporary and poorly informed administrators; lacking familiarity with agency programs, their decisions are necessarily based on preconceived notions which frequently hamper their overall effectiveness. Even under the most tranquil of circumstances, these conflicts lie just beneath the surface of federal employee relations.

The tension between career executives and political appointees has been particularly apparent within the Reagan administration. Top political officials have voiced fears that civil servants will sabotage policy initiatives to which they are unsympathetic, and career employees have complained of rising frustration in their dealings with politically appointed executives. Several Reagan appointees, including cabinet members, in tune with the administration's broad budgetary goals and political ideology, have openly been committed to the abolition of major programs or the dismemberment of entire agencies. Widespread layoffs in some agencies have also posed a direct threat to job security and undermined the morale of civil servants.

Such internal conflicts are to be expected in an administration proposing dramatic shifts in federal policy and more limited roles for federal bureaucrats. While the ultimate intent is not yet clear, the Reagan administration's general thrust in dealing with career employees appears to be directed toward the expansion of unilateral management rights at the expense of civil service protections. In controversies surrounding both hiring and firing procedures, the administration is seeking to loosen structured guarantees of merit and job security which lie at the heart of the civil service. These initiatives may never prove successful, but they reach well beyond the everyday tensions of the bureaucracy and raise the specter of a return to a more highly politicized spoils system of federal employment.

Getting In

The struggle to reconcile merit principles with equal employment opportunity has required adjustments in established civil service practices. Throughout the 1970s, the federal government attempted to modify its procedures for controlling employment consistent with affirmative action goals while remaining defensible on grounds of merit. The controversy regarding federal hiring procedures has often received greater attention than the limited number of jobs would appear to justify, for access to federal employment is both highly visible and symbolic. Continuing battles over the appropriate means for providing equal employment opportunity in the federal sector led to numerous revisions of hiring procedures, including the Reagan administration proposals to abandon the test used to qualify applicants for entry into professional, administrative, and clerical occupations in preference for greater management discretion in filling the ranks of the civil service.

To achieve hiring in line with merit principles, the federal government developed several entrance examinations to screen and help select federal job seekers. Uniform written exams administered to potential applicants on a periodic basis became characteristic of federal hiring procedures. Like similar aptitude tests developed by private firms, these instruments were designed to test deductive reasoning, mathematical ability, and reading comprehension. The most recent form of an "assembled" test was the professional, administrative, and clerical exam (PACE), which until its recent suspension was the basis for filling 118 entry-level positions. During fiscal 1980, nearly 67,000 applicants took the PACE; 44 percent passed (scores over 70), and 7 percent were hired from PACE registers. These totals represented a decline from their highest level in fiscal 1978, when over 135,000 people, about half of all applicants for GS entry positions, took the exam.

Standardized entrance examinations in the federal sector became the focus of concerns regarding the employment opportunities of minority groups because they did not produce results consistent with affirmative action goals. The development of the PACE itself was a response to a 1975 court ruling which held that the Civil Service Commission could not use a test that did not measure potential employee performance on a specific job, thus eliminating general intelligence tests.[3] This ruling resulted in a settlement with the plaintiffs that included monetary awards and an agreement to replace the federal service entrance exam (FSEE) then in use. A great deal of time and effort was devoted to the development of the PACE to achieve compliance with the court's order as well as with the guidelines on employee selection procedure.

Despite these efforts, however, the debate regarding possible discriminatory effects of standardized entrance exams continued. In a review of PACE scores, the General Accounting Office (GAO) found that 58 percent of white applicants and 12 percent of blacks passed the entry examination.[4] Normally a good chance of being selected for employment requires a score of 90 or above, a grade achieved by 16 percent of whites but only 0.2 percent of blacks taking the exam. The skewed results again called into question whether standardized exams fairly or adequately measure the capabilities of black job seekers, even though other federal hiring procedures might have enabled the government to reach its affirmative action goals. OPM defended the test on the grounds that high scores on the PACE correlated with good job performance. The agency also claimed that PACE scores reflected the composition of the applicant pool rather than test biases, arguing that the best-qualified black college graduates were hired by private employers and that black applicants retaking the exam in an effort to improve low scores may have been over-represented in the applicant pool.

These explanations of the poor performance of blacks failed to mollify minority groups, who continue to criticize OPM for a lack of sensitivity to racial and ethnic concerns. In spite of extensive effort to validate PACE during and after its development, critics attacked the test validation strategy claiming that the agency did not find ways to determine how blacks not passing the exam would perform in federal positions. This dissatisfaction with PACE eventually led to a second lawsuit in 1979 renewing the 1975 charge that it had a discriminatory effect in hiring minorities.[5] Without waiting for a court decision, the Carter administration negotiated a consent decree with the attorneys representing the complainants which required federal agencies to discontinue use of PACE for three to five years and to fill vacant positions with blacks and Hispanics in proportion to the applicant population. The decree, with modifications, was given final approval by the U.S. district court in November 1981.

The change of administration in 1981 triggered stiff opposition to the terms of the consent decree. Although Attorney General William French Smith refused to challenge the court order or to seek a renegotiated settlement, OPM director Donald J. Devine contended that the decree "imposes a heavy administrative and financial burden, and does not advance the affirmative employment aims of the plaintiffs."[6]

During its first year, the Reagan administration was reported to be considering a wide range of alternatives for implementing the decree, including: revision of the PACE, use of multiple PACE-like exams by individual agencies, continued use of the PACE but for filling fewer positions, or implementation of an affirmative action plan in addition to use of the PACE. It is doubtful that some of these would have received court approval, but there appeared to be numerous options open to the administration within the framework of the consent decree.

The course chosen by the Reagan administration deviated sharply from these varied proposals for modification of the PACE. On May 11, 1982, the Office of Personnel Management announced that the exam would be completely discontinued. In place of written exams, agencies would be free to exercise broad discretion in the selection of new workers. Federal agencies presumably will be encouraged to rely, to the extent possible, on internal promotion, lateral transfers, and referrals of laid-off workers from other departments to fill vacancies.

The abandonment of PACE has been hailed by some minority groups as a step toward a more effective affirmative action program in the federal government. In opting for a departure from quantifiable measures of test performance as the basis for civil service employment, OPM appears to have discarded hopes of striking a balance between affirmative action and strict adherence to the concept of the merit principle. The action left the Reagan administration open to the charge

113

that it used the equal employment controversy as a rationale for eliminating the constraints of objective hiring criteria and for broadening its own management prerogatives. As noted by Alan K. Campbell, OPM director under the Carter administration, the abolition of an entry-level test raises a host of dangers, with the potential for "movement away from objective selection . . . to other kinds of qualifications—ranging from political to nepotism to random selection."[7]

Approaches to the affirmative action problem other than the abandonment of PACE were available to the Reagan administration. For example, a plan put forward during the Carter administration would have used the written PACE to establish minimum qualifications, and then relied upon individual interviews and special considerations (such as outstanding grades) in making final selections. This proposal was based largely on hiring procedures for bank examiners employed by the Federal Deposit Insurance Corporation, in which the agency evaluates experience and skills in screening applicants with the minimum qualification of four years of college credit in accounting. The FDIC selection method raised the "pass rate" of blacks from 1 to 7 percent, still only half the proportion of hired white applicants.[8] Even if the FDIC hiring criteria which apply to only one job classification with fairly specific requirements are not directly applicable to the full range of jobs in the federal establishment, the agency's experience does suggest a middle ground in which affirmative action and merit hiring are not mutually exclusive.

The need for strict hiring quotas as mandated in the recent PACE consent decree will continue to be a topic of emotional debate. Some observers believe that any "adverse impact" on minorities must be assessed in the context of the federal government's overall affirmative action plan, as embodied in its uniform guidelines for equal employment. From this perspective, OPM has argued that the ratio of minority employment in federal jobs compares favorably with private employer experience and that alternative hiring practices have compensated for any adverse impact of PACE; blacks filled 17 percent of the positions in the sixteen most populous job classifications (accounting for three-fourths of all classified federal employees) for which PACE has been used.

In contrast, others have claimed that each aspect of selection and hiring procedures should be valid and without discriminatory effect, stressing that the rate of selection from the applicant population (data not collected by OPM) is more indicative of an adverse impact on minorities than statistics on total numbers employed. This debate was resolved by the U.S. Supreme Court in June 1982. The Court held that an adverse effect at any stage of the hiring process was illegal and could not be overcome by racial balance in the final selections. This will require all tests to be validated as predictors of job performance.[9]

There is no question that hiring minorities to compensate for past discrimination and to accelerate future advancement can be at odds with the concept of the merit principle on which civil service employment has been founded. But since the link between test success and job performance was never satisfactorily established by OPM, it could not claim that the concept of merit was in practice operative in federal personnel procedures. The compromises struck between the application of merit principles and equal employment goals must be the result of a careful balance between these laudable and important societal goals. One can only wonder whether any goal is justly served by the abandonment of valid, objective testing and the expansion of management discretion in federal hiring as proposed by the Reagan administration in the summer of 1982.

Treating Veterans and Women Differently

Since the passage of the 1944 Veterans' Preference Act, intended to compensate military personnel serving in World War II for the disruption of their careers and for disabilities suffered in combat, veterans have enjoyed favored treatment under federal hiring procedures. While support for recognition of military service has remained strong throughout the postwar era, the inevitable clashes among concerns for veterans' preferences, merit hiring, and equal employment has led to calls for limits on this special consideration.

Civil service law and regulations spell out the procedures for giving veterans a competitive edge in federal hiring. Applicants with prior military service secure advantages over their nonveteran counterparts in seeking federal employment in several ways. Extra points are added to the scores of veterans who passed the job entrance exams: 5 points for active service of 180 days or more, 10 if the veteran has a service-connected disability. In addition, disabled veterans placed on lists of eligible persons sent to agencies to fill a vacancy are automatically moved to the top of the list. In all positions veterans are rated ahead of those with the same score, and some jobs—those of guard, elevator operator, messenger, and custodian—are open only to veterans. In an effort to expand employment opportunities for women, President Carter supported the elimination of the veterans' preference as part of his 1978 civil service reform initiative. Veterans groups lobbied aggressively to retain favored treatment in hiring policies, and succeeded in limiting legislative changes to relatively minor revisions of the existing system. In its final form, the reform act eliminated the five-point preference for nondisabled veterans at or above the rank of major, allowed agencies to pass over veterans by offering written justification for their hiring decision to OPM, and entitled veterans with 30 percent or more disability to a review of agency denials of employment from civil service registers.

In the absence of more significant restraints on priority hiring of veterans, the preference system continues to loom as a major obstacle to the advancement of women employed by the federal government. More than 98 percent of America's 30 million veterans are males, limiting the ability of federal agencies to meet equal employment goals with respect to women.[10] Males account for three of every four federal administrative and professional employees, 60 percent of all technical employees, and 92 percent of all blue collar workers. While women comprise nearly 40 percent of the total GS work force, they enjoy less seniority and occupy proportionately fewer high-level positions than their male counterparts. Much of this employment record for women can be linked directly to veterans' preference procedures—the GAO has found that significant numbers of women, reaching as high as 20 percent on some employment registers, were kept out of federal jobs by the workings of the veterans' preference system.[11]

With males occupying at least 97 percent of all supervisory positions in the blue collar work force, women receive only 79 percent of male salaries in the Federal Wage System because relatively few of them have had the opportunity to advance into better paying job levels (Figure 6). Female GS employees fare even worse in salary comparisons, earning one-third less than the average male employee. This comparison does not take into account the female concentration in clerical jobs relative to men, who hold most of the management and professional positions. Lack of seniority and the remnants of discrimination permit similar wage inequities to linger in the private sector, while the veterans' preference has heightened the problems of ensuring access to equal employment and better paying jobs for women in the federal government.

In attempts to meet equal employment goals, agencies have developed ways of circumventing provisions for veterans' preference. A nonveteran

Figure 6. Women earned less than men in federal jobs in 1981

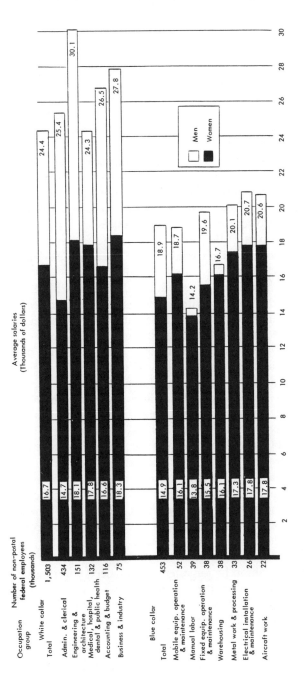

Source: Office of Personnel Management.

can be chosen over a disabled veteran from the three highest-ranked applicants if a written justification is approved by OPM, and some veterans' groups have charged that such "passovers" are routinely rubber stamped rather than scrutinized. A survey of such actions in 1976 and 1977 found that 73 percent of all passover requests were approved, but these cases accounted for only one percent of all appointments.[12] Veteran representatives have also charged that agencies reach below the top three applicants by arranging for another agency to request a certification of eligibles for a nonexistent vacancy, thereby "clearing the register" and enabling the agency with a genuine opening to hire an applicant with a slightly lower ranking.[13] These practices are not so prevalent as to negate the impact of the veterans' preference system, but they do illustrate agency efforts in circumventing federal policies favoring treatment for veterans.

Various proposals have been advanced to alter the preference system so that it would conflict less directly with merit hiring and equal employment opportunity for women. These options, which necessarily would have narrowed the competitive advantage enjoyed by veterans, included: limitation of preference to a one-time use for a single occupational category, or a specific period following military service; elimination of the placement of veterans ahead of nonveterans with identical scores (after preference points are added); and waiver of preference systems in agencies and/or occupations for which equal employment targets have not been reached. All of these options, however, were based on the premise that objective entrance examinations would generate rankings of applicants, a premise that has been undermined for some entry jobs by the Reagan administration's decision to abandon the use of the PACE and not replace it with a predictively valid test procedure.

Absent a method for rating applicants, it is not clear how the Reagan administration intends to implement veterans' preferences in federal hiring. President Reagan has advocated a reversal of his predecessor's effort to restrict use of veterans' preference, announcing that he "will not allow veterans to be forgotten in the federal government."[14] These priorities are also reflected in reduction-in-force (RIF) procedures, which continue to give veterans favored treatment and which currently have a more substantial negative impact on female employment than federal hiring practices.

With regard to veterans, the Reagan administration will have vastly greater discretion in structuring a preference system for veterans following the demise of standardized entrance examinations. The prior veterans' preference system was at least quantifiable and uniform, limiting the advantage of past military service to a finite margin in merit-based selection. Without test scores to modify, President Reagan's publicized commitment to federal hiring of veterans may be quickly transformed into yet another means for departing from merit principles and molding civil service employment to serve partisan ends.

Pruning the Bureaucracy

The Reagan administration's most dramatic and publicized initiative in federal employee relations has been the drive to reduce the size of the federal bureaucracy through RIFs. In recent decades, the stability of federal employment had become a significant attraction for many job seekers. This aura of job security has been shattered by President Reagan's determined effort to slash the number of workers on federal payrolls. Based on antigovernment ideology, the administration's personnel cuts have called into question the job security offered by existing civil service practices and have raised further fears that the ultimate intent is to obtain a freer hand in the removal of the nation's civil servants.

A number of complex procedures and statutory rights have been developed to insulate federal employees from capricious terminations in the case of overall personnel reductions. The procedures provide the structure for RIFs, but they do not preclude a degree of latitude for the exercise of personal judgment by federal managers. The definition of the "competitive area" in which job losses are to occur is pivotal in determining which workers are exposed to the threat of layoff, and the subjective guidelines for this decision may allow agencies to protect favored programs and personnel by not including them in the area. The consideration of performance ratings also enables managers to influence the RIF process. For instance, a manager might update performance appraisals prior to a RIF, giving favored employees an "outstanding" rating, equated with four years of seniority on the retention register. The agency may reassign or allow certain employees to "bump" outside designated areas as well, or it may convert some employees to part-time work, as long as they do not exceed full-time equivalent personnel ceilings.

The elimination of a position does not automatically result in the firing of the incumbent. Affected employees, if they have sufficient seniority or grade, may "bump" others within the competitive area out of their jobs. RIF-ed employees may also "retreat" to a similar position occupied by someone lower on the retention scale, or from which they have previously been promoted. If there are no open slots within the agency area, the employee has the choice of taking part in the displaced employee program (DEP) and/or the interagency placement program. The DEP is a mandatory program which gives top priority to RIF-ed employees for vacancies elsewhere in the agency and in other, unaffected agencies, for up to two years. The interagency placement program is a similar effort in which other federal agencies are required to request applications for open jobs from those affected by RIFs. Finally, the RIF-ed employee may appeal the firing to the Merit System Protection Board (MSPB), or may resort to a negotiated grievance procedure.

While federal employment has not been responsive to business cycles, large-scale reductions-in-force have occurred before the Reagan administration. For example, the Department of Defense used RIFs at the conclusion of wars in order to return to peacetime personnel levels. Excluding separations for cause, of the 250,000 affected by RIFs between 1964 and 1979, six of every ten were placed in other defense jobs or in other federal agencies; voluntary resignation and retirement accounted for nearly 30 percent of the separations, leaving about 10 percent who lost their jobs as a direct result of the RIFs.

The nondefense agencies also carried on RIFs before the Reagan era, but the number of employees affected was miniscule. As a direct result of RIFs, an estimated 1,300 people actually left the government in the five years preceding President Reagan's inauguration. In contrast, the explicit goal of the Reagan administration is to reduce total federal employment by 75,000 within its first three years. More than 10,000 employees were separated through reductions-in-force from January 1981 through August 1982. The full impact of the Reagan personnel cuts is difficult to assess at this early juncture. OPM claims that the effects of the RIFs on workers have been partially cushioned by its voluntary interagency placement and displaced employee programs.

The RIFs have also had far-reaching ripple effects. For every person RIF-ed three others are affected by bumping or retreating actions, altered work assignments, a process that often reduces pay and undermines employee productivity and morale. Moreover, evidence that the personnel reductions have been effective in reducing federal expenditures appears

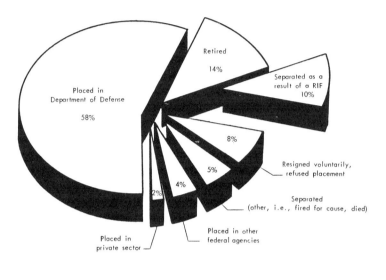

Figure 7. Between 1965 and 1979 there were 263,000
RIFs in the Department of Defense

Source: Department of Defense, Office of Civilian Personnel
and Labor Relations.

particularly weak. Although the RIFs have been advocated as a way to
save money, numerous costs cancel much of the savings. Direct costs
include severance pay (a week's salary for each of the first ten years of
service, and two weeks' pay for each of the next twenty-one years of
service), lump sum annual leave reimbursement, and unemployment
insurance and reimbursements for retirement contributions.

Perhaps more importantly, many indirect costs must be considered in
assessing the savings brought by RIFs—including the physical relocation
of transferred employees and support staff expenses, processing RIF actions, and defending RIFs in grievance arbitrations and Merit Systems
Protection Board appeals. Employees bumping or retreating to lower
paid positions are entitled to retain their higher pay for two years or
longer, delaying at least a portion of whatever savings might remain

121

after these direct and indirect costs have been tallied. Finally, while it may be impossible to quantify losses in productivity associated with employee transfers or low morale, the reassignment of workers to jobs in which they may have little experience or interest certainly takes its toll on the efficiency and morale of the federal bureaucracy.

The limited potential for reducing the government's wage bill is partially due to the nature of the RIF process itself. Both RIFs and forced early retirement carry unavoidable costs, and firing based on seniority and veteran status does not necessarily leave the government with the best employees. RIFs are not even effective in getting rid of "deadwood" in the upper levels of the bureaucracy because statutory protections allow such executives to escape termination of employment or to bump out those below them. Instead, to cite real, even though rare, examples, administrative personnel are transferred to secretarial positions or experts on aging programs are forced to work in the field of primary education. RIFs simply do not provide an effective vehicle for paring and pruning federal agencies.

These shortcomings have been exacerbated by the political realities of the attacks on the bureaucracy. Political support for RIFs is based on anti-Washington sentiments outside the nation's capital. An editorial appearing in a Georgia newspaper declared, "If a fear of RIF-decimated departments is afoot, maybe U.S. employees will work harder to make those departments—or their soft nooks, at any rate—seem worthy of a taxpayer's buck."[15] To avoid a reversal of the favorable attitude toward federal personnel cuts, RIFs have been concentrated in the Washington metropolitan area. Despite a GAO recommendation that the field structure is a "prime area for exploring ways to reduce unnecessary management levels, cut costs, and increase personnel efficiency,"[16] cutting personnel throughout the country runs a greater risk of raising opposition in Congress, and thus the District of Columbia area has suffered proportionately twice as many layoffs as any other metropolitan area. If RIFs could bolster government efficiency, the political overtones have most likely squandered their potential.

There are other indications that the Reagan administration has used RIFs as a political tool more than as a budgetary weapon. Personnel cuts have been virtually nonexistent in some agencies (such as the Department of Defense), while others less identified with the administration's ideological commitments (such as the Department of Labor and the Department of Health and Human Services) have lost a disproportionate number of employees. At least in part due to the seniority system, minorities have been RIF-ed at one and a half times the rate of nonminorities, and minority administrators have been three times as likely to be RIF-ed as their nonminority counterparts.

The cumbersome nature of RIFs and their questionable application in the federal work force have evoked increasing criticism of this approach to personnel and spending cuts. A congressional task force, admittedly partisan, summed up these frustrations: "If someone had to think of a way of reducing the size of government that totally disrupted the ongoing work of government, that costs the taxpayers money rather than saving it, that pitted employees against each other and against management, they couldn't have come up with a device more pernicious or ingenious than current RIF procedures."[17] Congressional opposition to the administration's personnel reductions has remained subdued, however, perhaps diffused by the sweeping nature of budget reductions proposed since President Reagan took office.

A few members of Congress, who place a high priority on job security in the federal establishment, introduced bills, backed by OPM Director Donald J. Devine, that would force agencies to furlough personnel rather than RIF them when feasible. Although furloughs also cause disruptions and loss of pay, the sponsors argued that their approach would produce immediate cost savings and would also allow a rational attrition plan to be developed and implemented. In addition, this alternative plan would give employees near retirement age the opportunity to reach their full term of service, eliminating the burden of early retirement payments. Finally, furloughs would provide enough lead time for the orderly transfer of people and program functions if an agency was to be phased out or its responsibilities diminished.

A blending of attrition and furloughs appears to offer an option that would meet the legitimate budgetary goals of the Reagan administration while avoiding the harsh disruptions of RIF procedures. According to OPM, attrition itself would create over 100,000 vacancies in the federal government based on the annual attrition rates that prevailed before the Reagan RIFs. While some of the vacated positions would have to be filled to preserve sound organizational structures, a predetermined attrition plan could compensate for a major portion of the 75,000 jobs now targeted for elimination. In the process, the federal government would avoid both unemployment payments and damaging effects of RIFs on employee morale and overall efficiency.

Brief furloughs rather than permanent layoffs could be implemented if planned attrition failed to reach personnel reduction goals. By placing a large number of workers on leave for a few days without pay, agencies could use this form of work sharing to reduce the impact of cuts on their employees and still achieve desired savings. Several agencies, including the Office of Personnel Management and the Bureau of the Census, chose to furlough employees for one day per biweekly pay period in order to make up for the budgetary cuts with a minimum of RIFs.

The Merit Systems Protection Board currently is responsible for final review authority over appeals of RIF proceedings. OMB Director David Stockman reportedly has asked the MSPB and OPM to consider a revision of these rules to give agencies the final say in RIF appeals.[18] While Stockman has stated that agencies "would have to provide a genuinely fair and objective appeal mechanism," the proposal would reverse the gradual movement in federal labor-management relations toward resolving disputes by independent agencies acting as neutral arbitrators. The intent certainly seems to be to give management a freer hand in interpreting and administering the troublesome RIF regulations.

More sweeping alterations of the existing RIF mechanism would require congressional approval, and yet there are indications that the Reagan administration may seek an authorization for expanded management prerogatives in personnel reductions. OPM Director Donald Devine has expressed interest in modifying or eliminating the seniority rules which he views as a major obstacle to efficient trimming and reorganization of the federal bureaucracy. As of mid-1982, details of such legislative changes have not been revealed, but the administration appears to be eyeing greatly expanded powers to terminate employees. Responding to political pressures, OPM Director Devine backed off from proposing his plans.[19] Consistent with their positions regarding entrance examinations and veterans' preferences, Reagan officials seem undisturbed by the prospect of undermining civil service protections and returning to a system in which federal employees are much more vulnerable to the whims and political motives of administration managers.

Relying on the Private Sector

The possible erosion of job security, stemming from expansion of management discretion in hiring and firing federal employees, may also be hastened by a reliance on the private sector. Contracting out and consulting have long provided alternatives to direct federal employment, and the use of private enterprises to carry out government functions when cost effective remains a popular concept. Yet aside from concerns about turning over governmental responsibilities to private individuals and companies, the amount and type of tasks shifted to outside the federal bureaucracy have direct implications for the job security of federal civil servants. Signs that the Reagan administration is seeking to press an ideological commitment to private enterprise by contracting out work even when estimated cost advantages may not justify such actions make job security in the federal establishment more tenuous.

Government contracting and consulting are restricted to circumstances in which it is not cost-effective to perform the work within a federal agency or to tasks that require expertise not available within an agency. However, the actual degree of reliance on the private sector changes with each administration. Although every president since Eisenhower has accepted the general parameters of official federal policy, each has interpreted and enforced it differently. President Ford, for example, ordered every agency to identify five projects that it could contract out, while President Carter reversed that directive and attempted to restrict use of private contractors by federal agencies. The General Accounting Office and others have repeatedly questioned the extent to which contracting decisions are based on objective cost comparisons rather than on political ideology.[20]

A major cause of the increasing reliance on private sector services by federal agencies has been the proclivity of the Congress to mandate the performance of additional functions without permitting agencies to expand their staffs. During the decade before fiscal 1981, real federal outlays rose by 54 percent, and expenditures for the purchase of goods and services rose 14 percent, yet federal civilian employment during the same period dropped about 5 percent. Federal agencies have responded to rigid personnel ceilings by contracting out many assignments previously performed by federal employees. The result has been gradually to displace potential jobs in federal agencies into the private sector.

The impact of contracting out on federal employment has been particularly visible within the blue collar work force. Since 1961, the number of blue collar employees in federal agencies has decreased by one-third, falling from 663,000 to 450,000 during that period. The Department of Defense, which employs two-thirds of all federal blue collar workers, eliminated nearly 8,000 positions between 1978 and 1980, claiming that this action would save the taxpayers $130 million over the next three years.[21] There is little doubt that this growing reliance on private firms through contracting has had significant and lasting consequences for federal blue collar employees in terms of lost job security, undermining the relevance of other statutory protections for the nation's civil servants.

As the erosion of job security has become increasingly apparent, the debate over cost savings associated with the contracting out of blue collar work has grown more controversial. Federal unions have challenged estimated savings cited by agencies, arguing that private firms underbid to gain government contracts and then claim cost-overruns once the government has turned over its operations and terminated or transferred its workers. The unions also have charged that, when real savings occur as a result of contracting, they are achieved at the cost of sacrificing pay standards and weakening quality controls by giving private firms incentives to cut corners in pursuit of greater profits. The General Accounting Office has raised other criticisms of federal contracting procedures as well, contending that clearer criteria should be specified as to the type of work best suited for private contractors. GAO also indicated that many commercial and industrial activities operated by federal agencies at an annual cost of $18.5 billion should be more closely examined for potential contracting out to private firms.

Notwithstanding these concerns, the Reagan administration appears prepared to press its shift to private-sector contracting beyond areas of clear cost efficiency. Legislation supported by the administration would prohibit federal agencies from engaging in commercial or industrial activities if such work could be performed by private firms at "fair and reasonable" prices—in effect mandating contracting out of work even in cases where private sector costs are not lower than federal costs but simply are "reasonable." Opposition in Congress to such an acceleration of contracting out based on the perceived threat to government employees is already evident, and the adoption of amendments limiting contracting in certain circumstances suggests that legislative proposals backed by the administration are unlikely to win approval in the near future. Yet the thrust of the Reagan administration's initiative provides another example of its willingness to sacrifice the job security of civil servants for the fulfillment of its antigovernment bias.

Consulting practices are not nearly so politically appealing as contracting out and do not create the same sharp conflicts with federal employment, but they do raise other legitimate policy concerns. Although OMB loosely defines consulting as "those services of a purely advisory nature relating to the governmental functions of agency administration and management," outside consultants may in some cases actually determine policy under the guise of providing data collection and analysis. Personnel ceilings have forced many agencies to farm out work to consultants that would more appropriately fall within the purview of permanent federal employees, including program development, research, and evaluation. In the process, it often becomes difficult to distinguish between advice and policy control, since some consultants filter information and limit options as they attempt to structure alternatives and recommendations. Perhaps more importantly, heavy reliance on consultants reinforces beliefs that civil servants are not capable of carrying out the full complement of agency responsibilities, and disguises the true size of the federal work force by shifting work from explicit government payrolls into consulting contracts.

In contrast to trends in contracting out, political sentiments regarding consulting almost universally favor limitations on the use of outside personnel. Expenditures for consultants have posed an easy target for ridicule by congressional budget cutters, as reflected by Senator William Proxmire's golden fleece awards and reemphasized by the 1981 budget reconciliation act requiring a $500 million slash in the overall federal consulting bill. Nevertheless, these constraints on consulting practices have not been coupled with an acknowledgment of the legitimate personnel needs of federal agencies, and Congress has succeeded only in painting executives into a tighter corner by restricting one of the few remaining options for meeting agency personnel requirements. This course in itself may not jeopardize the jobs of federal employees, but it certainly will not make the demands placed on civil servants any more reasonable.

Reactions to Change

Viewed collectively, recent developments in hiring and firing procedures can only serve as a source of consternation for those who are committed to the preservation of an independent civil service at the federal level. In seeking greater discretion in the selection and termination of federal employees, the Reagan administration threatens to weaken the central principles of merit and job security which provide the foundation for the civil service structure. Existing protections for federal workers are not likely to disappear overnight and administration initiatives requiring congressional approval may well be stymied by congressional opposition. At the very least, however, the unusually persistent efforts by Reagan officials to meet the administration's political and ideological goals must be viewed as a significant challenge to the integrity of the independent civil service.

Given the emerging pattern of administration policies, federal unions have been notably silent regarding issues of hiring and firing. No doubt the relative lack of labor opposition to proposed changes in hiring and firing procedures is at least partially due to the continuing uncertainty as to the broader direction and intent of administration initiatives in these areas. Yet the muted response of federal unions is also a reflection of the very real sense in which these issues create internal divisions within the union membership—pitting whites against blacks, veterans against women, senior civil servants against newly hired personnel, and public sector workers against their private sector counterparts. With regard to federal hiring and firing practices, union members reflect a multitude of competing and conflicting interests which often prevent them from speaking with a strong and unified voice in response to administration proposals.

The clearest illustration of the divisiveness of hiring issues is found in the almost total absence of union involvement in the debate over federal affirmative action policies. With no responsibility to represent the interests of applicants yet to be hired, unions have avoided choosing sides in implicit conflicts between white and minority job seekers or between veterans and women, believing their involvement could only alienate portions of their constituency. Unions might accurately view the abandonment of entrance examinations as a dangerous departure from the concept of merit principles and an indirect threat to the job security of all federal workers. Reactions to even this step may be restrained by the understanding that neither PACE nor its predecessor exam were predictively valid, and some steps had to be taken to comply with equal employment opportunity in hiring. Thus, most federal labor leaders have little choice but to watch the debate over selection procedures from the sidelines, since their roles focus on practices affecting incumbent workers once they have been hired but not before.

Federal unions of course are unified in their opposition to layoffs in the federal establishment, and the more militant organizations have attempted to arouse public opposition to the Reagan administration's personnel reductions. However, unions have discovered they have little leverage in attempting to forestall RIFs; although about 67 percent of negotiated agreements contain references to RIF procedures, most require only notice to the union or that statutory rules be followed.[22] A sampling of those agreements found that about 27 percent require union consultation, but only a handful of union contracts include provisions for union participation in the determination of the competitive area, the key first step which influences the allocation and scope of personnel cuts. Until 1981 unions apparently placed little emphasis upon RIF procedures and possibly did not consider that RIFs deserved priority consideration.

In a direct effort to block RIFs, the National Treasury Employees Union failed to provide sufficient evidence to convince a U.S. district court that RIFs would hamper the ability of federal agencies to carry out their duties.[23] Most unions have advocated the use of furloughs instead of permanent layoffs, and yet even this posture has placed unions in a bind because furloughs affect all workers equally, regardless of seniority, thereby conflicting with organized labor's traditional emphasis on seniority and strict employee rights. Other union interventions have added to the disruption and disarray. For example, in fiscal 1982 the Department of Labor was required by contract to serve 120-day advance notice for any RIF. Unable to determine in advance the 686 employees who would eventually be terminated, the department served notice on all the 2,460 employees in the affected units. Finally, federal unions may be able to prevent overt manipulation of federal employees through either grievance arbitration procedures, or through a case-by-case approach before a Merit Systems Protection Board. The latter is applicable if grievance/arbitration remedies are not available or if discrimination is alleged. Yet the chances of a timely hearing before the MSPB, overwhelmed with appeals and plagued by budget cuts, offers scant hopes of significant success in battling widespread RIFs.

Prospects for a meaningful union role in contracting and consulting practices appear no brighter. Federal union opposition to contracting out exists, but a significant proportion of the blue collar workers most affected are represented by larger, private sector affiliates in which they comprise only a small portion of the total membership. The private sector members may be the beneficiaries of contracting out and are not likely to oppose work transfers from the government to private employees. Consulting practices attract less union attention because they usually augment rather than replace the efforts of federal employees, and have the greatest impact on upper-level personnel most of whom are not eligible for union representation. Given the political popularity of a reliance on the private sector and the desire of federal unions to avoid direct confrontations with their private sector counterparts, organized labor in the federal establishment has remained fairly silent in discussions of contracting out and consulting procedures.

With unions largely unable to represent a unified work force on issues affecting hiring and firing, it is understandable that resolution of controversies relating to these matters has been repeatedly left to Congress and the White House. In virtually all cases, the most interested parties—minority, women's, and veterans' groups, as well as irate taxpayers—are outside the federal employment system and exert their influence through political lobbying efforts. Political leaders are thus forced to choose between competing groups and conflicting goals, balancing concerns for management efficiency against claims for redress of social inequities and appeals to the ideals of an independent civil service based on merit. The mediation of these diverse demands through compromise and confrontation provides no guarantees of sound management policies in the federal sector, but it offers the only practical means of making inherently normative decisions as to who should be hired and fired in the federal establishment.

It remains to be seen whether President Reagan will seek greater discretion in personnel matters in a vigorous and comprehensive fashion, and whether Congress will defend the independent civil service. Historically, Congress has been wary of civil service procedures that leave open the possibility of political manipulation by the chief executive and his appointees. Much will depend on how blatantly the administration presses for the withdrawal of protections based on principles of merit and seniority, and on how successfully critics of such proposals can untangle the interrelated issues of affirmative action, budgetary restraint, and fundamental assurances of job security and competence in the civil service. What is clear is that the incentives for the administration to wield its influence over civil servants will remain strong, and that only Congress can attempt to strike a proper balance between employee rights and management needs to maintain a competent and secure federal work force in the decades ahead.

8

Making the Civil Service Work

The lot of the federal civil servants is not a happy one. The object of political attacks, the supposed cause of many of the nation's woes, and the hapless victims of misguided public opinion, they are as a group among the most maligned employees in America.

The picture of the briefcase-toting bureaucrat is pervasive in the public mind. Constant caricatures of overpaid and underutilized federal workers in the media have had the effect of creating an almost wholly negative public image for them. The reality behind the image of public employees who plan national defense, process social security checks, minister to disabled veterans, and administer farm aid programs is rarely perceived.

A Political Scapegoat

Politicians of every stripe have capitalized on the poor image of the federal bureaucrat. For years it has been acceptable practice for candidates to run against the "Washington establishment" which is said to be responsible for the many economic and social woes of the nation. President Carter came to office in 1977 in part on the strength of his promise to reform the bureaucracy. He identified civil servants with "inefficiency, ineptitude, and even callous disregard for the rights and feelings of ordinary people" and promised to reorganize and streamline the bureaucracy.[1] Candidate Reagan was even more blunt; his expressed intention was to trim the federal wasteline by slashing the federal employment rolls.

Of late, the presumably swollen wage bill has been blamed in part, at least, for high deficits. The effects of stagnant economic performance by the private sector have been channeled into indignation over the allegedly excessive pay of federal workers. As a result two administrations have been able to cap top federal pay and limit annual increases to levels well below targets set through the statutory pay system. The increasingly serious disruptions in management created by this scapegoating of federal workers have not dampened the enthusiasm of political leaders because the attacks on Washington bureaucrats continue to play well in Dry Gulch.

Even basic assaults on the customary personnel practices of merit selection and job security have triggered little opposition from Congress. As the Reagan administration appears to pursue broader management discretion in federal hiring and firing, only those groups most directly affected by entrance examinations and RIFs have voiced concern about the potential for renewed politicization of the federal employment system. The evidence of partisan manipulation is not yet apparent, however, to trigger a backlash in public opinion. In sum, the political climate hardly bodes well for the civil servant.

Recent developments in the federal employment system under the Reagan administration represent attempts to reverse nearly two decades of steady gains in worker protections within the federal establishment. The growth of federal unions, the emergence of impartial collective bargaining procedures, and the tentative implementation of a pay-setting system based on objective criteria have all contributed to the expansion of individual employee rights in the federal establishment. Civil servants now have access to neutral third parties for grievances and statutory appeals as a means of preventing infringements upon their rights, and they also can band together to elect representatives of their own choice in pursuit of common interests. Traditional labor-management structures for federal employees are far more constrained than those available in the private sector, but the attempt to remove by civil service statutes at least some issues from political arenas certainly has strengthened the more basic protections.

In reversing the trend toward independent arrangements for resolving disputes in federal labor relations, recent actions by the Congress and chief executive have weakened the federal employment system. Ceilings on executive pay have left senior managers increasingly discouraged, and many have left the upper ranks of government for more lucrative positions in private industry or for generously indexed retirement benefits. Finally, reductions in force have caused employee morale to plummet while wreaking havoc upon concepts of efficient organization and personnel management. The results of these diverse political interventions serve the interests of neither the public nor federal workers and managers.

It will never be possible to insulate federal labor relations completely from political considerations, nor should that be the goal of employment policies. In the private sector as well as the federal government, labor and management occasionally find it advantageous or necessary to pursue political solutions to their problems. Outside interest groups (including taxpayers, minorities, veterans, and women) who perceive a stake in the workings of the federal employment system preclude in many cases the resolution of disputes at the bargaining table and turn to judges and politicians to advance their causes. This development is not only unavoidable, but it is also fully appropriate given the principles of democratic government and the dual role of political leaders as traditional managers and elected representatives.

Unfortunately, the revisions of the federal employment system launched in 1981 have gone beyond the inevitable search for political legitimacy and the minimization of political conflict. The departures from principles of fair pay, merit selection, and job security are rooted in rigid ideological perspectives rather than in a careful balancing of federal worker interests and management needs.

Attacks on federal civil servants may continue to be good politics, and that fact alone will pose as a major limiting factor in considering proposals for realistic change within the federal establishment. Yet the goal of responsible social policy must be to expand the use of impartial institutions and procedures through which competing demands can be weighed and policies adopted in a fair and efficient manner.

Toward a Rational System

The preceding chapters explore current federal employee relations problems and weigh options for future remedies. In most cases, no simple policy prescriptions are apparent, if only because there is a lack of political consensus to support effective change. Yet a case can be made for a series of adjustments in the federal employment system which, although not radical in nature, would preserve both legitimate worker rights and the central principles of a competent and independent civil service.

For those committed to the negotiating rights already in place in the private sector, it is tempting to argue for the establishment of a parallel system of collective bargaining to resolve most issues in federal employee relations. Union-management negotiation could be the basis for setting wages, hours, position classifications, and working conditions, similar to procedures adopted by many state governments. Most settlements would require only pro forma ratification by the Congress, relieving Congress from dictating terms of federal employment, but without restricting the legislative prerogative of setting policy. This would open to federal workers the opportunity to have a voice in the determination of employment policies through the presence of their representatives at the bargaining table.

Although greater reliance upon collective bargaining in the federal establishment might offer an improvement over the present disarray, such a scenario looms highly unlikely in the foreseeable future. The political risks of surrendering direct legislative control, the prospect of rising wage bills under a bargaining system, and the negative image of public employee negotiations all pose major obstacles to the acceptance of broad bargaining rights in the federal government. Of equal importance, federal employees show no signs of militancy and even interest necessary to induce policymakers to expand the role of collective bargaining. As long as the hands of federal unions are tied by the relative apathy and resignation of their members, sweeping revisions to enhance worker rights in the federal employment system do not appear to be in the offing.

In the absence of a radical overhaul of the employment system, several modifications are needed to keep it functioning with reasonable fairness and effectiveness. These marginal improvements would not alter the basic concepts upon which the civil service is founded, but instead would serve to bring theory and practice back into alignment. Fulfillment of this agenda for change would not halt many of the debates regarding the appropriate boundaries of federal policy. It would prevent, however, more serious erosion of the principles that have guided the civil service for nearly a century.

Compensation in the federal sector provides one of the most obvious areas for revision, as politicians now routinely approve pay levels far below the mark of comparability with the private sector. The concept of comparability offers a seemingly objective standard by which to gauge "fair" and "adequate" compensation and thereby carries broad political appeal, and neglect of the recommendations has shorn the current process of its legitimacy. Unless political leaders opt for a different basis for adjusting federal compensation, the existing structure for implementing the comparability principle requires pressing attention.

Improvements in the comparability system must begin with a commitment to some measure of total comparability which accounts in a prudent fashion for fringe benefits as well as wages. The specific formula used to compare such benefits is open to debate, but it is shortsighted to assert that workers ignore pensions, health insurance, and other benefits in making job decisions. The attempt to consider fringe benefits in comparability measures should not include, however, intangible benefits such as power, security, and prestige which can not be quantified in a reliable way.

In conjunction with the revision of comparability measures, the present division in federal compensation between locally determined blue collar pay scales and nationally set white collar wages should be altered to reflect the realities of labor market competition. The distinction between blue and white collar pay is highly arbitrary, more a function of social convention than of established links between specific occupations and either national or local labor markets. For this reason, studies ranging from the first Hoover Commission in 1949 to the Rockefeller Report in 1975 have called for a more rational correlation between the nature of individual occupations and the geographic bases of relevant wage scales. In particular, the determination of lower-level white collar pay on a local basis seems warranted.

To reflect the wide fluctuations in pay for technical and clerical workers across localities found by the 1975 Rockefeller Commission, lower grades of the current GS payroll should be melded into the blue collar system (FWS) and paid according to local wage scales. Workers from entry-level through GS-11 or -12 (journeyman's rate) could be treated in this manner, with the remainder of the schedule and the Senior Executive Service retained on a national pay scale. A number of technical issues would require attention in such a reorganization, including determination of the cutoff occupation between local and national scales and assurances of some separation between the highest locally set wages and the lowest national wage rate. Yet these problems are not insurmountable, and the division of the white collar payroll would create a compensation system that more closely matches the market in which recruitment occurs.

The most basic threat to the effectiveness of federal pay systems is not in their technical design and implementation but rather in the weak commitment of political leaders to their observance. Complaints regarding the accuracy of comparability measures often provide excuses for deviating from the dictates of pay systems, and in this sense revisions to measure total comparability and to determine white collar wages on a local basis are important to the credibility of comparability as an appropriate reference point for federal pay. However, such changes will be meaningless if policymakers are not committed to making the system work. Continual politicization of pay issues only wastes the substantial public funds needed to conduct comparability surveys and undermines the legitimacy of the pay process.

If federal workers are not soon to be granted the right to bargain over wages, the authority of the impasses panel should be expanded to resolve labor-management disputes arising under the restricted scope of bargaining. "Show cause" hearings, time limits on negotiations, and greater flexibility for the imposition of contract terms by the impasses panel all offer potential for modest improvement in this regard. Given the continuing ban on strikes and wage bargaining, hidden agendas will remain a troublesome part of labor-management relations in the federal establishment.

Beyond these statutory restrictions, the collective bargaining arrangements appear to be functioning reasonably well, although controversies on agency shop and duration of negotiations deserve attention. Management objections to unlimited official time payments for negotiations are persuasive, and yet in the absence of agency shop fees union representatives would be precluded from bargaining on a par with their management counterparts. Ideally, the ban on agency shop fees should be reconsidered, for there appears to be no justification for treating federal workers differently from private sector employees in this area. With political opposition likely to prevent unions from marshaling the financial resources to bear some portion of negotiation costs, however, the most practical alternative is to limit the period for negotiations (and thus also reduce outlays for travel and official time payments), and provide for intervention by the Federation Mediation and Conciliation Service and the impasses panel after the deadline is reached.

The most serious disruptions in the federal employment system are surfacing in areas of hiring and firing, often in ways that threaten the basic principles of the civil service. The exact intent of the Reagan administration in revising hiring and firing procedures is not clear, but the effect of its proposals would be to expand management discretion at the expense of worker protections from political manipulation. Even if one accepts the administration's concerns as valid, there appear to be far preferable and less dangerous remedies for the shortcomings of existing hiring and firing regulations.

The decision to abandon standardized entrance exams appears based on political expediency. A sounder approach to the dilemma would be to construct a series of valid, performance-predicting tests for similar jobs. This would require several tests for the 118 occupations for which the PACE entrance exam was used.

Finally, a smaller and efficiently organized work force can be achieved without the abuse of worker rights and civil service protections. Attrition, transfers, and early retirement all can be used to pare the size of the federal work force, and furloughs, as a last resort, can also slash the federal wage bill while preserving jobs. Legislation requiring both agencies and unions to negotiate alternatives to RIFs, with intervention by the impasses panel in the event that agreement cannot be reached, also may offer a more equitable and objective process for allocating necessary personnel reductions.

When layoffs are unavoidable, some limits on bumping and retreating rights should be instituted to prevent the placement of employees in positions for which they are overqualified and overpaid. More sweeping revisions to elevate some vaguely defined concept of efficiency above considerations of seniority, veterans' preference, or minority status should be rejected as an almost certain path to political favoritism in federal employment.

Efficiency and Worker Rights

It is ironic that efficiency in the federal establishment has always been linked with unfettered management prerogatives. The private labor relations system, with its extensive collective bargaining rights, is built on the assumption that worker involvement is a precondition for the efficient resolution of labor-management disputes, and that concerns not addressed at the bargaining table will result in troublesome disruptions of the workplace. While only one of every five workers has joined unions and the collective bargaining system is not warmly embraced by all private employers, its orderly structure and use of impartial referees are usually acknowledged as an effective means of reconciling conflicting management and labor interests. Any hint of a compulsory shift toward unilateral management discretion for the sake of efficiency would only lead to greater chaos and confrontation in the private sector.

With the ability to impose many terms of employment by fiat, policymakers traditionally have ignored the potential gains in efficiency that a more comprehensive system of collective bargaining might bring to the federal government. Congressional opposition has stemmed from concerns that expansions in the role of organized labor would unleash more strident worker demands not easily quieted or contained, and that expanding the scope of bargaining rights would restrict the ability of politicians to choose expedient solutions to federal employment problems.

The Hatch Act prohibition against employee involvement in federal elections illustrates the reluctance of elected officials to permit a stronger voice for federal workers. Congress had tended to confuse the elimination of the spoils system with the rise of self-awareness among federal employees. In many areas, only a fine distinction exists between protecting civil servants from political manipulation and preventing them from promoting their legitimate interests. With collective bargaining narrowly prescribed and the right to strike totally denied, federal employees and their unions frequently have no alternative but to resort to political action to achieve their goals. In this context, the presumed protection offered by the Hatch Act can be seen as yet another way of controlling dissent among federal workers, legislating submission in spite of the inefficiencies inherent in a disgruntled or, at best, apathetic work force.

It is necessary to dispel the myth that worker rights and collective bargaining are contrary to efficiency in government. Orderly procedures for determining the conditions of federal employment—including meaningful opportunities for worker participation and recourse to neutral arbiters—would go a long way toward improving morale in the civil service and ensuring that disputes are resolved in a fair and efficient

138

manner. An expanded collective bargaining system may bring some additional costs, especially if wages and layoffs are brought to the negotiating table. Yet it is important to recognize that the nation's taxpayers may already bear the burden of these costs indirectly, through the loss of competent workers and the absence of appropriate incentives in the federal employment system. In a democratic society committed to the participation of all its members, the fuller involvement of civil servants would respond both to our aspirations for fair play and to the orderly administration of the nation's affairs. It is time to begin work on a more efficient approach to federal employee relations.

Notes

1. Managing in the Public Interest

1. Jack Stieber, "Collective Bargaining in the Public Sector," in Lloyd Ulman, ed., *Challenges to Collective Bargaining* (Englewood, N.J.: Prentice-Hall, 1967), p. 81.

2. Alan K. Campbell, U.S. Congress, Senate Committee on Governmental Affairs, *Hearing on the Federal Employees Compensation Reform Act of 1979* (Washington: Government Printing Office, August 2, 1979).

2. The Rise of Federal Unions

1. Commission on Organization on the Executive Branch of the Government, Final Report, 1949 (Washington: Government Printing Office, 1949).

2. Jack Stieber, "Collective Bargaining in the Public Sector," in Lloyd Ulman, ed., *Challenges to Collective Bargaining* (Englewood, N.J.: Prentice-Hall, 1967), p. 69.

3. The President's Task Force on Employee-Management Relations in the Federal Service, "A Policy for Employee-Management Cooperation in the Federal Service" (Washington: Government Printing Office, November 30, 1961), p. 4.

4. James L. Stern, "Unionism in the Public Sector," in Benjamin Aaron, Joseph R. Grodin and James L. Stern, eds., *Public Sector Bargaining* (Madison, Wis.: Industrial Relations Research Association, 1979), pp. 54-62; and U.S. Office of Personnel Management, "Union Recognition in the Federal Government" (Washington: Government Printing Office, 1981).

5. Anthony F. Ingrassia, cited in James W. Singer, "The Limited Power of Federal Worker Unions, *National Journal,* September 30, 1978, p. 1547.

6. Richard B. Freeman and James L. Medoff, "New Estimates of Private Sector Unionism in the United States," *Industrial and Labor Relations Review,* January 1979, p. 171.

7. Anthony F. Ingrassia, "Labor Relations Challenges for Management in the '80s," address before the All-Department of Defense Labor-Management Relations Conference, Memphis, Tennessee, January 23, 1980, p. 18.

8. *Government Employee Relations Report,* Reference File (Washington: Bureau of National Affairs, 1982), p. 51:530.

9. Murray B. Nesbitt, *Labor Relations in the Federal Government Service* (Washington: Bureau of National Affairs, 1976), p. 71.

10. Marcus H. Sandver, "The Financial Resources of Federal Employee Unions," *Monthly Labor Review,* February 1978, pp. 49-50.

11. *Government Employee Relations Report,* September 1, 1980, p. 5.

12. James Singer, "The Limited Power of Federal Worker Unions," *National Journal,* September 30, 1978, p. 1550.

13. *Government Employee Relations Report,* September 1, 1980, p. 5.

14. *National Treasury Employees Union v. Bureau of the Public Debt,* 3 FLRA 120 (1980).

15. *National Treasury Employees Union v. Nixon,* 492 F.2d 587 (D.C. Cir. 1974).

16. *National Treasury Employees Union v. Fraser,* 428 F. Supp. 295 (D.C. Cir. 1976).

17. M.J. Fox, Jr. and Marvin Judah, "National Treasury Employees Union: Description of a Federal Employee Union," *Journal of Collective Negotiations in the Public Sector,* vol. 9, no. 1, 1980, p. 49.

18. Office of Personnel Management, *Union Recognition in the Federal Government, 1980* (Washington: Government Printing Office, 1981), pp. 22-23.

19. Victor Gotbaum, "Collective Bargaining and the Union Leader," *Public Workers and Public Unions,* ed. Sam Zagoria (Englewood, N.J.: Prentice-Hall, 1972), p. 80.

3. The Emergence of Collective Bargaining

1. Presidential Review Committee on Employee-Management Relations in the Federal Service, *Study Committee Report and Recommendations* (Washington: Government Printing Office, August 1969), p. 1.

2. Joel Havemann, "Can Carter Chop Through the Civil Service?" *National Journal,* April 23, 1977, p. 616.

3. "Carter Given Reorganization Authority," *Congressional Quarterly Almanac 1977,* p. 749.

4. "Can Reorganization be 'Painless'?" *National Journal,* April 23, 1977, p. 618.

5. FLRA rules and regulations; subpart B, section 2424.11 and Carl C. Clewlow and David H. Green, "The Compelling Need Doctrine" in *Labor Management Relations Service* (Englewood, N.J.: Prentice-Hall, October 23, 1979), pp. 3263-5.

6. William Ford, *Congressional Record* (daily edition), September 13, 1978, p. H9650.

7. *Association of Federal Government Employees AFL-CIO, Local 2875 and Department of Commerce,* 5 FLRA 55 (1981).

8. *National Treasury Employees Union and Department of Health and Human Services, Region X, Seattle, Washington,* 5 FLRA 93 (1981); and *Association of Civilian Technicians, Pennsylvania State Council and the Adjutant General, Department of Military Affairs, Commonwealth of Pennsylvania,* 3 FLRA 8 (1980).

9. U.S. Court of Appeals for the District of Columbia, *Department of Defense, Army-Air Force Exchange Service, Dix-Maguire Exchange, Fort Dix, N.J. v. Federal Labor Relations Authority*; and *Department of Defense, Department of the Air Force, Air Force Logistics Command, and Air Force Logistics Command, Wright-Patterson Air Force Base, Ohio v. Federal Labor Relations Authority* (cases 80-1119 and 80-1351, 1981).

10. *National Labor Relations Board Union and National Labor Relations Board,* 3 FLRA (1980).

11. *NTEU and Internal Revenue Service,* 3 FLRA 112 (1980).

12. *Association of Civilian Technicians, Delaware Chapter and National Guard Bureau, Delaware National Guard,* 3 FLRA 9 (1980).

13. *AFGE, AFL-CIO, and Department of Defense, Army-Air Force Exchange Service, Dix-Maguire Exchange, Fort Dix, N.J.,* Court Case No. 80-1119; cited in note 9.

14. *AFGE Local 1968 and Department of Transportation, St. Lawrence Seaway Development Corporation, Massena, New York,* 5 FLRA 14 (1981).

15. Case no. 80-1351 cited in note 9.

16. *AFGE, Local 32 and Office of Personnel Management, Washington, D.C.,* 3 FLRA 120 (1980), and *NTEU and Department of Treasury, Bureau of Public Debt,* 3 FLRA 119 (1980).

17. *AFGE, Local 1968 and Department of Transportation, St. Lawrence Seaway Development Corporation, Massena, New York,* 5 FLRA 14 (1980).

18. Henry H. Robinson, *Negotiability in the Federal Sector* (Ithaca, N.Y.: Cornell University and American Arbitration Association, 1981).

19. William Ford, *Congressional Record* (daily edition), October 14, 1978, p. H13608.

20. Cited in Jack Stieber, "Collective Bargaining in the Public Sector," in Lloyd Ulman, ed., *Challenges to Collective Bargaining* (Englewood, N.J.: Prentice-Hall, 1967), p. 80.

21. Robert S. Summers, *Collective Bargaining and Public Benefit Conferral: A Jurisprudential Critique* (Ithaca, N.Y.: Institute of Public Employment, New York State School of Industrial and Labor Relations, 1976); and Harry H. Wellington and Ralph Winter, "The Limits of Collective Bargaining in Public Employment," *Yale Law Journal,* June 1969, pp. 112-27).

22. Sanford Cohen, "Does Public Employee Unionism Diminish Democracy?" *Industrial and Labor Relations Review,* January 1979, p. 189.

4. The Role of the Peace Keepers

1. Herbert J. Lahne and Edward H. Ghearing, "Federal Employee Bargaining Unit Determinations," *Monthly Labor Review,* July 1964, pp. 763-64.

2. "Report and Recommendations of the FLRC on the Amendment of E.O. 11491 as Amended" (Washington: Government Printing Office, 1975), p. 1.

3. Clyde M. Webber, "Why the Executive Order Should be Replaced by Legislation," *The Bureaucrat,* Special Issue 1973, p. 96.

4. *Panama Canal Commission,* 5 FLRA 20 (1981).

5. *DOT, Bureau of Government Financial Operations,* 1 FLRA 62 (1979); *Department of State, Passport Office Chicago Passport Agency,* 1 FLRA 33 (1979); *Virginia, Washington, D.C.,* 1 FLRA 55 (1979); and esp. *U.S. Army Commos and Electronics Material Readiness Command, Fort Monmouth, N.J.,* 1 FLRA 75 (1979).

6. *National Marine Fisheries, Service, Southeast Fisheries Center, Miami, Fla.,* 3 FLRA 79 (1980); and *The Alaska Railroad, Federal Railroad Administration, Department of Transportation,* 3 FLRA 105 (1980).

7. *Trident Refit Facility, Bangor, Bremerton, Washington, and International Association of Machinists Local 282 and AFGE and Bremerton Metal Trades Council,* 5 FLRA 84 (1981).

8. *International Communication Agency and NFFE Local 1418; and ICA and AFGE Local 1812,* 5 FLRA 19 (1981).

9. Committee for Economic Development, *Improving Management of the Public Work Force* (New York: Committee for Economic Development, 1978), p. 102.

10. *United States Naval Weapons Center, China Lake, California,* 1 FLRC 405 (emphasis added).

11. *Georgia National Guard,* 2 FLRA 92 (1980), *Army and Air Force Exchange Service, Base Exchange, Fort Carson, Fort Carson, Colorado,* 3 FLRA 95 (1980), and *New York National Guard,* 9 FLRA 2 (1982).

12. *National Guard Bureau, Massachusetts Air National Guard,* 3 FLRA 132 (1980).

13. *U.S. Department of Commerce, National Oceanic and Atmospheric Administration, National Weather Service, Eastern Region, and National Weather Service Employees Organization,* MEBA, AFL-CIO, 5 FLRA 43 (1981).

14. *Policy Statement,* 2 FLRA 31.

15. Anthony F. Ingrassia, "Labor Relations Challenges for Management in the 80s," address to the Third Annual All-Department of Defense Labor-Management Relations Conference, Memphis, Tennessee, January 23, 1980, pp. 3, 11.

16. 7 FLRA No. 105 (1982).

17. Federal Labor Relations Authority, "Report on Case Handling Developments of the Office of the General Counsel" (Washington: Federal Labor Relations Authority, March 1981), p. 4.

18. *San Antonio Air Logistics Command, Kelly Air Force Base, Texas and AFGE Local 1617,* 5 FLRA 22 (1981).

19. *Federal Correctional Institution and AFGE Local 2052,* 8 FLRA 111 (1982).

20. D. S. Chauhan, "The Political and Legal Issues of Binding Arbitration in Government," *Monthly Labor Review,* September 1979, p. 36.

21. Howard Solomon, U.S. Congress, House Committee on Post Office and Civil Service, "Hearings on Oversight before the Subcommittee on the Civil Service," April 29, 1980, p. 11.

22. Howard Gamser, U.S. Congress, House Committee on Post Office and Civil Service, "Impasses Resolution in the Federal Sector," February 24, 1982.

23. Thomas A. Kochan, *Collective Bargaining and Industrial Relations* (Homewood, Ill.: Richard Irwin, 1980), p. 385.

24. *Department of the Air Force, Civilian Personnel Branch, Carswell Air Force Base, Texas, and AFGE Local 1364,* 5 FLRA 7 (1981).

25. *Picatinny Arsenal, U.S. Army Armament Research and Development Command, Dover, N.J., and National Federation of Federal Employees, Local 1437,* 7 FLRA 109 (1982).

26. *American Federation of Government Employees, San Francisco Region and Office of Program Operations, Social Security Administration, San Franciso Region,* 7 FLRA 98 (1982) is one recent example.

27. *Veterans Administration Hospital and AFGE, Lodge 2201,* 4 FLRA 57 (1980).

28. *American Federation of Government Employees Local 2811, and U.S. Government District Office, Social Security Administration, St. Paul, Minnesota,* 7 FLRA 97 (1982).

29. Federal Mediation and Conciliation Service Memo No. 82-1, March 8, 1982.

30. Office of Personnel Management, Office of Labor-Management Relations, "A Survey of Negotiated Grievance Procedures and Arbitration in Federal Post Civil Service Reform Act Agreements," September 1980, p. ii.

5. The Attempt to Rationalize Federal Pay

1. "Occupations of Federal Blue-Collar Workers," Office of Personnel Management Pamphlet 59-14, October 1980, p. 4.

2. Harry A. Donovan, "A New Approach to Setting the Pay of Federal Blue-Collar Workers," *Monthly Labor Review,* April 1969, p. 30.

3. *The Federal Wage System,* Federal Facts Services 7 (Office of Personnel Management, June 1980).

4. Thomas W. Gavett, "Policymaking and the Role of Labor Statistics," *Monthly Labor Review,* September 1971, p. 39.

5. 5 *U.S.C.* Section 5301(a)(3).

6. Felice Porter and Richard L. Keller, "Public and Private Pay Levels: A Comparison in Large Labor Markets," *Monthly Labor Review,* July 1981, pp. 22-26.

7. George L. Stelluto, "Federal Pay Comparability: Facts to Temper the Debate," *Monthly Labor Review,* June 1979, p. 20.

8. Merit Systems Protection Board, "A Report on the Senior Executive Service" (Washington: Merit Systems Protection Board, September 1981), pp. 55-57.

9. Mike Causey, "Top Technical Jobs Are Going Begging," *Washington Post,* July 26, 1981, p. B2.

10. George Borjas, *Wage Policy in the Federal Bureaucracy* (Washington: American Enterprise Institute, 1980), esp. table 11, p. 39.

11. *The Civil Service Retirement System,* Federal Facts Series 3 (Office of Personnel Management, December 1979).

12. Comptroller General, "Total Compensation Comparability for Federal Employees" (Washington: General Accounting Office, Report FPCD 80-82, September 1980), p. 4.

13. "A Decade of Federal White Collar Pay Comparability, 1970-1980," Report from the Advisory Committee on Federal Pay (Washington: Government Printing Office, January 15, 1981), p. 28.

14. Comptroller General, "Proposal to Lower the Federal Compensation Comparability Standard Has Not Been Substantiated" (Washington: General Accounting Office, Report FPCD 82-84, January 26, 1982), p. 4.

15. *Staff Report of the President's Panel on Federal Compensation* (Washington: Government Printing Office, January 1976), p. 87.

6. Fair Pay and an Efficient Work Force

1. Walter Fogel and David Lewin, "Wage Determination in the Public Sector," *Industrial and Labor Relations Review,* April 1974, pp. 410-31.

2. Sharon Smith, *Equal Pay in the Public Sector: Fact or Fantasy?* (Princeton, N.J.: Princeton University Press, 1977).

3. Joseph F. Quinn, "Wage Differentials among Older Workers in the Public and Private Sectors," *Journal of Human Resources,* Winter 1979, pp. 41-62.

4. William R. Bailey, "Pay Differentials between Federal Government and Private Sector Workers," *Industrial and Labor Relations Review,* October 1977, p. 78.

5. James E. Long, "Are Government Workers Overpaid? Alternative Evidence," *Journal of Human Resources,* Winter 1982, pp. 13-131.

6. Civil Service Commission, "Study of Private Enterprise Pay Rates for Positions Equivalent to GS-14/18" (Washington: Civil Service Commission, June 1974).

7. Douglas B. Feaver, "Pay Ceiling Creates Brain Drain at the Top," *Washington Post,* July 24, 1981, p. A-11.

8. Comptroller General, letter to Senator Ted Stevens, chairman of the Subcommittee on Civil Service, Post Office, and General Services, November 10, 1981, reprinted in the *Congressional Record* (daily edition), November 12, 1981, p. H238.

9. Committee for Economic Development, *Improving Management of the Public Work Force* (New York: Committee for Economic Development, 1978), p. 103.

10. Merit Systems Protection Board, Office of Merit Systems Review and Studies, "A Report on the Senior Executive Service" (Washington: Government Printing Office, September 1981).

11. Merit Systems Protection Board, "The Other Side of the Merit Coin" (Washington: Government Printing Office, February 1982), p. 4.

12. Mike Causey, "A Pay Surprise Coming in October," *Washington Post,* July 21, 1981, p. B-2.

13. Lloyd G. Nigro, "Attitudes of Federal Employees toward Performance Appraisal and Merit Pay: Implications for CSRA Implementation," *Public Administration Review,* January/February 1981, pp. 84-86.

14. "Three Studies, Federal Managers Tell Subcommittee Merit Pay Has Problems," Bureau of National Affairs, *Government Employee Relations Report,* July 27, 1981, p. 16.

15. Naomi Lynn and Richard E. Vaden, "Public Administrators: Some Determinants of Satisfaction," *Bureaucrat,* Summer 1979, pp. 66-70.

16. Merit Systems Protection Board, Office of Merit Systems Review and Studies, "A Report on the Senior Executive Service" (Washington: Government Printing Office, September 1981), p. 16.

17. Eugene H. Becker, "Analysis of Work Stoppages in the Federal Sector, 1962-81," *Monthly Labor Review,* August 1982, pp. 49-53.

18. Lawrence M. Jones, David G. Bowers, and Stephen H. Fuller, *Management and Employee Relations within the Federal Aviation Administration,* vol. 1 (Washington: Institute for Social Research, March 17, 1982).

19. Statement of Ronald W. Haughton, "Impasses Resolution in the Federal Sector," Hearings before the U.S. Congress, Subcommittee on Investigations, House Post Office and Civil Service Committee, February 24, 1982.

20. *Staff Report of the President's Panel on Federal Compensation* (Washington: Government Printing Office, January 1976), p. 148.

21. *Staff Report of the President's Panel on Federal Compensation* (Washington: Government Printing Office, January 1976), p. 35.

22. Roger Schmenner, "The Determination of Municipal Employee Wages," *Review of Economics and Statistics,* February 1973, pp. 83-90; James L. Freund, "Market and Union Influences on Municipal Employee Wages," *Industrial and Labor Relations Review,* April 1974, pp. 391-404; and David Shapiro, "Relative Wage Effects of Unions in the Public and Private Sectors," *Industrial and Labor Relations Review,* January 1978, p. 202.

7. A Return to the Spoils System?

1. U.S. Congress, House Post Office and Civil Service Committee, *Violations and Abuses of Merit Principles in Federal Employment* (Washington: Government Printing Office, December 30, 1971).

2. Committee for Economic Development, *Improving Management of the Public Work Force* (New York: Committee for Economic Development, 1978), p. 93.

3. *Douglas v. Hampton,* 512 F.2d 976 (D.C. Cir. 1975).

4. Comptroller General, "Federal Employment Examinations: Do They Achieve Equal Opportunity and Merit Principle Goals?" (Washington: General Accounting Office, Report FPCD 79-56, May 15, 1979), p. 10.

5. *Luevano v. Campbell,* No. 79-0271 (D.C. Cir. 1979).

6. "PACE Consent Decree," memo from Donald Devine to Cabinet Secretaries, reprinted in *Government Employee Relations Report,* January 25, 1982, p. 63.

7. Mike Causey, "PACE Is Abolished to Correct Its Bias," *Washington Post,* May 12, 1982, p. C2.

8. William Raspberry, "Screening for Jobs without Screening Out Minorities," *Washington Post,* November 25, 1981, p. A21.

9. *Connecticut v. Teal* (1982).

10. Dean K. Phillips, "The Case for Veterans' Preference," *Stranger at Home: Vietnam Veterans since the War* (New York: Praeger, 1980), p. 352.

11. Comptroller General, "Conflicting Congressional Policies: Veterans' Preference and Apportionment vs. Equal Employment Opportunity," (Washington: General Accounting Office, Report FPCD 77-61, September 29, 1977).

12. Statement of Alan K. Campbell, "Civil Service Reform," Hearing before the U.S. Congress, House Post Office and Civil Service Committee (Washington: Government Printing Office, 1978), p. 815.

13. Statement of Ronald W. Drach, "Veterans Preference and Equal Employment Opportunity," Hearing before the House Post Office and Civil Service Subcommittee on Civil Service, October 6, 1977, pp. 6-8.

14. Quoted in Philip Shandler, "Veterans Get New Message on Job Front," *Washington Star,* July 15, 1981.

15. *Augusta Chronicle,* May 7, 1982.

16. General Accounting Office, "Supervisor to Non-Supervisor Ratios," Report B-200576, September 30, 1980, p. 5.

17. Karlyn Baker, "'Reagan Roulette' and Its Impact," *Washington Post,* February 28, 1982, p. 1.

18. Mike Causey, "Changes Considered in RIF, Pay Protests," *Washington Post,* May 25, 1982, p. C2.

19. *Government Employee Relations Report,* "OPM Backs Off from Rule Changes," July 26, 1982, p. 14.

20. Comptroller General, "Civil Servants and Contract Employees: Who Should Do What for the Federal Government?" (Washington: General Accounting Office, Report FPCD 81-43, June 19, 1981), p. 26.

21. Karlyn Baker, "The Job Ax," *Washington Post,* August 26, 1981, p. C1.

22. Office of Personnel Management, "A Survey of Reduction in Force Provisions in Federal Labor Agreements," Office of Labor-Management Relations, Report No. 81/11, April 1981, p. 1.

23. Karlyn Baker, "Civil Servants Ask Court to Bar RIFs," *Washington Post,* September 18, 1981, p. B12.

8. Making the Civil Service Work

1. Jimmy Carter, "Making Government Work Better: People, Programs, and Process," *National Journal,* October 9, 1976, p. 1448.

Index

About the Authors

Sar A. Levitan is Research Professor of Economics and Director of the Center for Social Policy Studies at The George Washington University. He has written more than thirty books. Fourteen of those have been published by Johns Hopkins, including his most recent volume, *What's Happening to the American Family?* (coauthored with Richard S. Belous). *Alexandra B. Noden* is a former research assistant at the Center for Social Policy Studies and is now studying law.